NEW ORLEANS HOUSES

Corinthian column

NEW ORLEANS HOUSES
A HOUSE-WATCHER'S GUIDE

LLOYD VOGT

PELICAN PUBLISHING COMPANY
GRETNA 1997

First printing, June 1985
Second printing, January 1987
Third printing, January 1989
Fourth printing, May 1992
Fifth printing, February 1997

Library of Congress Cataloging in Publication Data

Vogt, Lloyd
  New Orleans houses.

  Bibliography: p.
  1. New Orleans (La.) – Dwellings – Guide-books.
2. Architecture, Domestic – Louisiana – New Orleans –
Guide-books. I. Title.
NA7238.N5V64   1985   728'.09763'35   84-9541
ISBN 0-88289-299-1

Manufactured in the United States of America
Published by Pelican Publishing Company, Inc.
1101 Monroe Street, Gretna, Louisiana 70053

This book is dedicated to the front porch, one of the jewels of New Orleans architecture for more than two hundred years, now fallen victim to the technological advances of the twentieth century.

Ionic column

CONTENTS

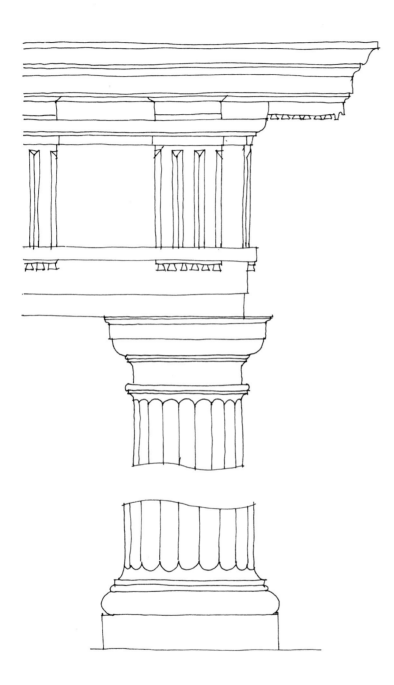

Doric column

ACKNOWLEDGMENTS

I would like to thank the following for their assistance, guidance, and encouragement in the development of this book: Louis Bisso, Mary Ranlett, Peter Schmidt, Melinda Jordan, Ann Hessel, Connie Mercer, Debbie Taylor, the staff of the Historic New Orleans Collection, my editor Frumie Selchen, my wife Mary Ellen, and my sons Darren and Ian.

I would especially like to thank Robert W. Heck, Alumni Professor of Architecture at Louisiana State University, for his advice throughout the evolution of *New Orleans Houses,* but more importantly for the inspiration his teaching of architectural history has provided to me and countless others.

NEW ORLEANS HOUSES

INTRODUCTION

The city of New Orleans is one of America's greatest outdoor museums. Its streets boast a treasury of architectural types and styles of local origin as well as magnificent examples imported from throughout the United States and other parts of the world and adapted to the city's subtropical climate and unique geographical conditions.

New Orleans has always been a city of conflicts. Her struggles began with the founding of the settlement on a site more suitable for mosquitoes and alligators than for human habitat. Through the years she has battled the river, hurricanes, floods, fires, political corruption, riots, and epidemics. She was built on swampland, much of it below sea level, necessitating construction of one of the world's great drainage systems. Yet despite these hardships her citizens have continued their tradition of living life to its fullest. New Orleans is a proud city, determined to preserve her cultural heritage—a heritage derived from a diversity of influences including French, Spanish, English, African, Caribbean, American, German, Irish, Italian, and Latin American. Over the years these cultures have merged to create an ambience unmatched in America.

To understand New Orleans architecture is to begin to understand the city itself, for the buildings a culture erects are an expression of that culture's history, values, and tastes. Man's dreams, aspirations, and techniques for survival are all clearly reflected in the buildings he leaves behind, from the most utilitarian to the most lavish.

New Orleans Houses has been written as a "house-watcher's guide," to enable the layman to identify the style of a house, understand its origins, date its construction within ten or fifteen years, and place it in its historical context. Armed with this knowledge, house-watchers can learn to understand the aes-

thetics, history, and values of bygone eras and gain an appreciation of the streetscape which we so often take for granted.

This book examines the houses of New Orleans by exploring two main characteristics: type and style. Building types are determined by form and room arrangement, while styles are identified by ornamental embellishments and by such characteristic building elements as windows and doors. After a brief discussion of types and styles, the city's houses are explored chronologically. Each historical period is discussed in terms of major events, personalities, and growth patterns; for each a map of the city indicates the area previously settled and the developing areas during that period. A description of the house styles popular during the period follows, with sketches of typical houses constructed in those styles.

The houses illustrated here represent the most common styles and associated types found throughout the city. These sketches of houses are character sketches, developed by studying numerous examples of a particular style and creating a composite of those characteristics most commonly associated with the style in New Orleans. In a few cases an actual house was sketched if it represented either an especially excellent example or one of the city's few remaining examples of a style. This method has been generally avoided to prevent the singling out of a particular house as the "perfect example" of a style.

Numerous illustrations accompany the text, and a glossary of the architectural terms used is also included.

The architecture of New Orleans, like the city itself, is unique, and this uniqueness is waiting to be discovered. It is my hope that this book will provide the basic knowledge necessary for understanding and appreciating the houses of our historic and beautiful city, and that it will help provide the spark for a lifetime of enjoyable house-watching.

HOUSE TYPES

Fourteen house types have been selected as the most common in New Orleans; the criteria used for classifying types are form and room arrangement. Given the enormous variety of houses in the city, the choice of fourteen is to some extent a subjective one. Moreover, many houses, primarily the more recent ones, do not fit any previously classified type: in these cases no specific type is mentioned. The types and styles included here were chosen because they best explain the evolution of the city's residential architecture.

In most cases the popularity of a building type spanned more than one period and that type was therefore associated with more than one style. The New Orleans shotgun house type, for example, was popular from the antebellum period through the early twentieth century, and was built in the Greek Revival, Italianate, Eastlake, Bracket, Neoclassical Revival, and Bungalow styles, whereas the entresol house type had a much more limited period of popularity as a Creole expression during the post-colonial era.

The following are the major house types in the city in the chronological order in which they developed:

FRENCH COLONIAL PLANTATION HOUSE

Constructed as plantation houses from the early 1700s to the early 1800s, these rectangular structures were raised above ground-level cellars with the main floor on the second level and storage below. A gallery on the second level was on at least two sides and sometimes all four. A steep hipped roof was generally pierced by dormers on either two sides or on all four. The number of rooms varied, but the floor plan never included hallways. The smaller houses often had three rooms positioned side by side, while the larger houses might have two parallel rows of three rooms each. Small rooms called *cabinets*—commonly used for storage—were usually positioned at the rear outer corners of the house. Each room on the second level had french doors opening onto the gallery. This house type was influenced by the buildings of the West Indies and represents a blending of French and Spanish influences.

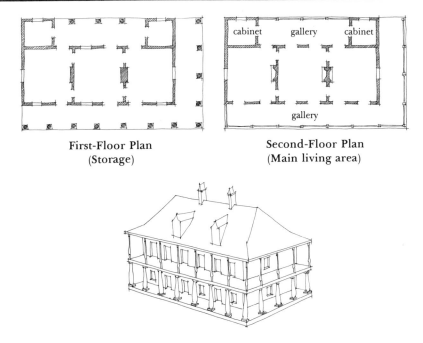

First-Floor Plan
(Storage)

Second-Floor Plan
(Main living area)

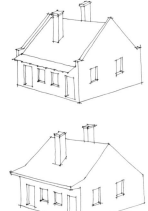

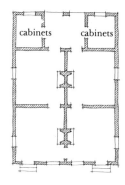

cabinets   cabinets

CREOLE COTTAGE

Creole cottages, which may have originated in the West Indies and been introduced to New Orleans by refugees from Haiti, were popular in the city from about 1790 to 1850. These straightforward and unornamented buildings were the most common houses in New Orleans during the early 1800s. They are found in greatest numbers in the Vieux Carre and Faubourg Marigny, where it was not unusual for a builder to erect an entire row of five or six identical structures.

In most cases Creole cottages, square or rectangular in shape, fronted directly on the *banquette* (sidewalk), and were raised only one or two steps above it. The typical plan consisted of four rooms arranged symmetrically, each approximately twelve to fourteen feet square, with two additional small *cabinets* in the rear outer corners. One *cabinet* generally housed a spiral staircase to the attic, which was normally used as a sleeping room, while the other was used for storage.

Two variations on this plan exist but are not nearly as common. The two-bay cottage was a half Creole cottage with two rooms, one behind the other, and a *cabinet* in the rear. The three-bay cottage had the same room arrangement as the two-bay with the addition of a side entrance hall. Most of the three-bay cottages were built in the 1840s and 1850s.

Most Creole cottages had either gable or hip roofs. The gable-roofed cottage, the more common of the two, appeared in three versions, differentiated by the treatment of the front facade roof extension that projected three or four feet over the sidewalk. The first version, the *abat-vent,* consisted of an almost flat roof extension supported by iron bearers cantilevered from the facade at the roof line. In the second version the extension was formed by a slight upturning (canting) of the roof, and in the last the extension was incorporated into the roof line.

Outbuildings, generally two stories high, were built in the backyards of most Creole cottages.

CREOLE TOWNHOUSE

The Creole townhouse, found primarily in the Vieux Carre, became a common house type as the city was rebuilt after the great fires of 1788 and 1794 and was popular until about the mid-nineteenth century.

These rectangular structures—detached, semidetached, or constructed in rows—were two to four stories high, with balconies at the second and sometimes third levels enhanced by delicate wrought-iron railings. A steeply pitched roof with roof dormers was also a common feature.

The first level had arched openings, a distinguishing feature of the type, with multilight french doors protected by vertical-board shutters. A paneled doorway in one of the side openings led to a very narrow flagged or bricked pedestrian passageway similar to the carriageway of the porte-cochere townhouse (see below) but much too narrow for the passage of a carriage. Beyond this passageway was an enclosed stair gallery positioned between the main house and a service wing attached to one side in the back. A wide arch in the rear wall at the first level opened onto the courtyard. The first-floor plan featured double parlors one behind the other, parallel to the passageway, or one large room. The second level usually included a large front room spanning the entire width of the house, with a second room situated to the rear. When there were more than two floors the upper floors were generally identical to the second.

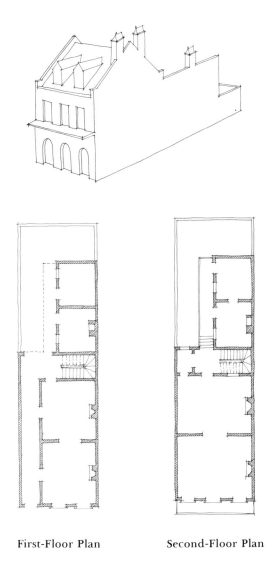

First-Floor Plan   Second-Floor Plan

17

PORTE-COCHERE TOWNHOUSE

A two-, three-, or four-story building common in the Vieux Carre from about 1800 to 1850, the porte-cochere townhouse featured a carriageway entrance (normally arched and placed to one side of the facade) with a bricked or flagged passage leading to a courtyard in the rear. The ground floor was often used as a commercial shop, and consisted of two rooms of approximately the same size, one opening to the street facade, the other to the rear stair hall. The stairway, placed in the corner, led to the upper levels, which were used as living quarters.

The service wing was either attached to one side of the rear of the house, forming one wall of the enclosed courtyard, or situated on the rear lot line parallel to the house.

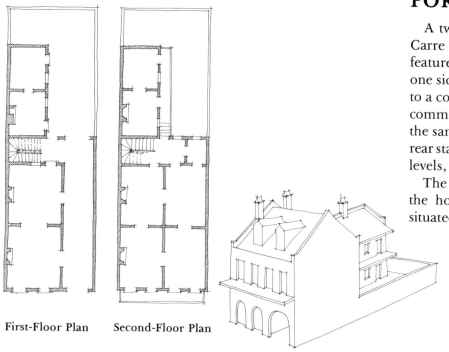

First-Floor Plan   Second-Floor Plan

ENTRESOL HOUSE

Constructed in the Vieux Carre during the postcolonial period, the entresol house was characterized by a second floor unperceived from the outside. This floor, a low-ceilinged storage area separating the ground-floor commercial space from the upper-level living quarters, was normally located at the spring point of the first-floor arched openings. The fanlights of the ground-floor openings served as windows to allow light into the storage area.

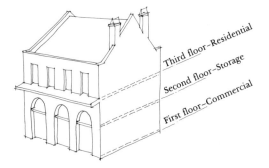

Third floor–Residential
Second floor–Storage
First floor–Commercial

18

OUTBUILDING

Outbuildings—support buildings for the main house—were a common feature of urban dwellings from the early 1800s until approximately 1860. Before 1830 they were usually completely detached from the main structure, forming the rear or side wall of a flagstone- or brick-paved courtyard. After 1830 it was common practice to attach the outbuilding to the rear of the main house. In the 1850s the popularity of outbuildings began to decline and they were gradually incorporated into the design of the main structure.

Outbuildings varied in height from one to three stories; two stories were the most common. The floor plan generally included two or three rooms, one room deep, on each level. The ground level housed the kitchen (separated from the main house because of the heat generated there and the threat of fire), possibly a dining area, and storage rooms. Small bedrooms on the upper levels were used primarily by the servants or by the older children of the family.

Since in most cases outbuildings were constructed either at the side or back of the property, it is common to find the outbuildings for two houses back to back, sharing a center wall, with the end gables extending above the roof line and forming a fire wall. A shed roof pitching into the courtyard usually projected about three or four feet, covering an upper-level wooden gallery with a wooden balustrade constructed of simple, square balusters.

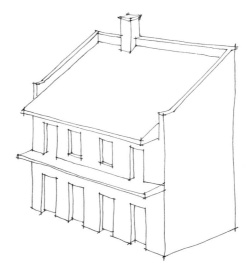

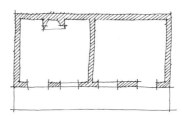

Second-Floor Plan

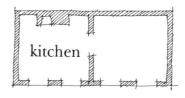

First-Floor Plan

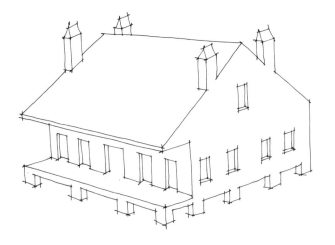

AMERICAN COTTAGE

American influence on the Creole cottage resulted in a five-bay, center-hall cottage. Similar in profile to its Creole predecessor with gabled sides, this American cottage, inspired by the Georgian houses of the Northeast, consisted of four rooms arranged symmetrically but separated by a center hall. The fireplaces and chimneys were located on outside walls, whereas the Creole cottage featured interior-wall fireplaces.

Many of these houses were raised a full story above the ground with a broad gallery stretching across the entire front facade at the second level. Such cottages, generally referred to as raised cottages, had the main living area on the upper level, with the first level used primarily for storage. The American cottage made its first appearance in New Orleans in the 1820s and was popular from about 1830 to 1870.

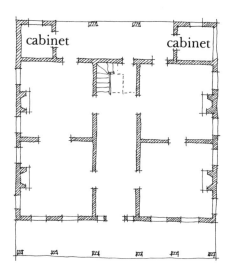

AMERICAN TOWNHOUSE

Another house type influenced by the architecture of the Northeast, the American townhouse appeared in New Orleans during the 1830s. It differs significantly from the Creole townhouse because major emphasis is placed on entrances, and because of the incorporation of interior side hallways connecting interior stairs. The sidehall plan usually had a three-bay facade with two or three rooms aligned from front to rear, parallel to an interior sidehall with a stairway to the upper levels. American townhouses were two to four stories high and were frequently constructed as row houses. A two-story service wing was attached to one side at the back of the house.

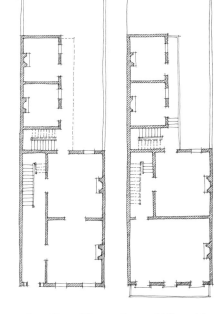

First-Floor Plan   Second-Floor Plan

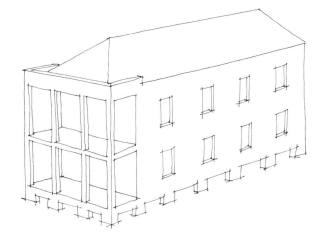

DOUBLE-GALLERY HOUSE

Many New Orleans houses, especially the sidehall American townhouse and the two-story shotgun double (see below), can also be categorized as double-gallery houses.

This double-gallery type is a two-story building that evolved during the antebellum period. Its distinguishing feature is broad galleries across the front facade at both levels, supported by either pillars or columns.

21

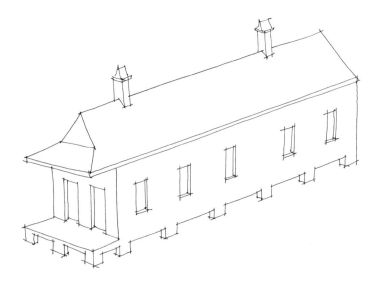

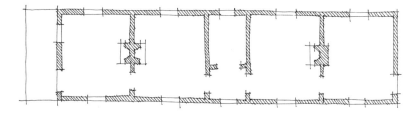

SHOTGUN SINGLE

The shotgun single is a rectangular house with all the rooms arranged directly behind one another in a straight line, front to back. The term *shotgun* is said to have originated because of the notion that if a shotgun were fired through the front door all the pellets would leave through the rear door without hitting anything.

Shotgun houses are usually of wood-frame construction with weatherboard siding, raised two or three feet on brick piers. The origin of this house type is uncertain, but it has often been conjectured that the concept was imported from Africa or Haiti. The shotgun is thought to have developed in rural areas rather than as an urban expression; shotgun singles are very common throughout the countryside surrounding New Orleans.

The shotgun house type first appeared in New Orleans during the 1830s. The early shotguns generally had hipped roofs on the front and rear, or a hipped front and gabled rear. They were built close to the ground and abutting the sidewalk, with a shallow roof overhang in the front. During the 1850s shotguns with front galleries, set back from the sidewalk, became popular.

Shotgun singles were built in a number of subtypes:

The two-bay single without halls is usually three to five rooms deep. Chimneys are most often located at the center ridge of the house, on a dividing wall between two rooms. Two other two-bay singles are the lateral-wing type and the lateral-wing type with side gallery.

The more spacious three-bay shotgun single features an entrance hall to one side, usually two rooms deep, with the front two rooms used as a double parlor. In this situation fireplaces are located on the outer walls. This room arrangement suggests that this subtype was influenced by the sidehall American town-house. Three-bay shotguns are usually four or five rooms deep.

SHOTGUN DOUBLE

The shotgun double is a two-family house composed of two shotgun singles joined under one roof and separated by a center wall. Fireplaces are generally centered in the dividing wall and serve two rooms. Occasionally they are placed in a corner, where they serve four rooms.

The shotgun double is a very common house type in New Orleans. It was first built in the city around 1840, and remained popular for approximately one hundred years.

The four-bay double (two two-bay singles) is by far the most common subtype, but five-bay doubles (a two-bay single and a three-bay single) and six-bay doubles (two three-bay singles) are also scattered throughout the city.

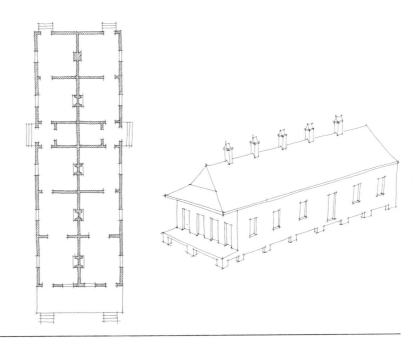

CAMELBACK

The camelback is a shotgun single or double with one story in the front and two in the rear. The origin of this house type is unknown. It has often been suggested that it developed because taxes were levied on the basis of the height of a house along the streetfront, rather than its height in the back. However, it is entirely possible that the camelback developed in New Orleans as the direct descendant of the Creole cottage, for in essence the Creole cottage is a two-room shotgun double: when a two-story outbuilding is relocated from the rear of a property and attached to the back of a cottage, thus becoming incorporated into the main building, the structure becomes a camelback shotgun double. Camelbacks were popular from the 1860s to the early 1900s.

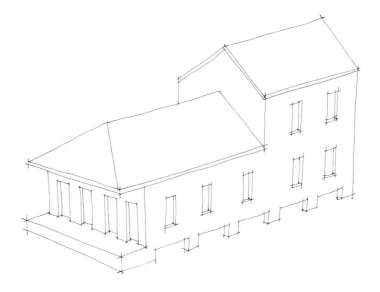

23

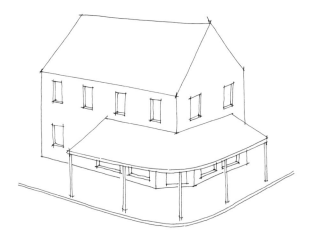

CORNER STOREHOUSE

One feature of neighborhood land-use patterns in nineteenth-century New Orleans was the utilization of corner lots for commercial establishments. The corner storehouse that resulted is a combination commercial-residential building featuring a commercial area on the ground level and residential space above. The commercial space usually housed a grocery store, shop, restaurant, or bar. Floor plans varied to meet the needs of the individual establishment. A distinguishing characteristic of the type is a wraparound corner canopy projecting over the sidewalk at the first level. This canopy is usually supported by wooden pillars or by colonnettes of iron or turned wood.

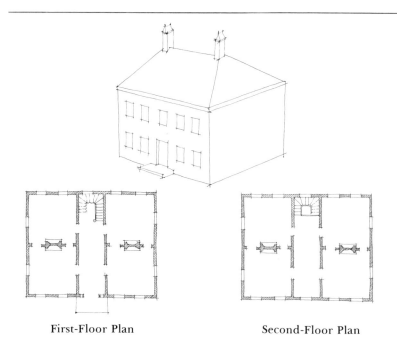

First-Floor Plan   Second-Floor Plan

GEORGIAN

The design of the Georgian house type is based on principles of formal composition. Squarish in shape, this five-bay, two-story house has a central hall flanked by two rooms of approximately the same size on each side. The plan is symmetrical, with a medium-pitched hipped or side-gabled roof. The second floor was usually identical to the first in Georgian Colonial houses, but the type was not common in New Orleans until the Georgian Colonial Revival, when bathrooms were incorporated into the second-floor plan.

The American cottage is a one-story version of the Georgian plan.

24

HOUSE STYLES

Rather than discussing every house style used in American domestic architecture, this book focuses on those most commonly found in New Orleans. Some styles that enjoyed considerable popularity in other parts of the country—including Federal, Stick, Shingle, and Prairie—were for one reason or another never popularized here and are therefore not included, even though isolated examples do exist in the city.

Each style is discussed in the context of the era during which it became popular. Some styles do not fit neatly within a period. In these cases they have been placed during the period with which they are most closely associated. The following are the major historical periods in the development of New Orleans and the architectural styles associated with them:

THE COLONIAL PERIOD (1718–1803)
The French Colonial style

THE POSTCOLONIAL PERIOD (1803–1830)
The Creole style

THE ANTEBELLUM PERIOD (1830–1862)
The Greek Revival

THE VICTORIAN PERIOD (1862–1900)
The Gothic Revival
The Italianate style
The Second Empire style
The Eastlake style
The Bracket style
The Queen Anne style
The Richardsonian Romanesque style

THE EARLY TWENTIETH CENTURY (1900–1940)
The Georgian Colonial Revival
The Neoclassical Revival
The Tudor Revival
The Bungalow style
The Spanish Colonial Revival

THE MODERN PERIOD (1940–)
The International style
The Suburban Ranch style

Although most New Orleans houses can be readily identified as belonging to a particular style, many others cannot. There are several reasons for this phenomenon. Some houses are unique in their design, never having conformed to any particular style. Others are composites of two or more styles, frequently because they were constructed during a transitional period as the popularity of one style waned and that of another grew. (The transition from Greek Revival to Italianate in the 1850s is a good example of this situation: many houses constructed during this period have characteristics of both styles.) Moreover, through the years many houses have been modified in appearance through additions, renovations, partial demolition, remodeling, replacement of rotted wooden elements such as balustrades and columns, or attempts at updating and conforming to the fashion of the times. This process continues in many neighborhoods today, along with the practice of reusing salvaged materials such as old doors, mantels, and stained glass in new construction.

In addition, in recent years there has been a tendency to construct replicas of earlier house styles. In the majority of cases these attempts at copying suffer from serious flaws, leaving numerous telltale signs of contemporaneity. Ceiling heights in the new houses are more often eight feet than the original twelve

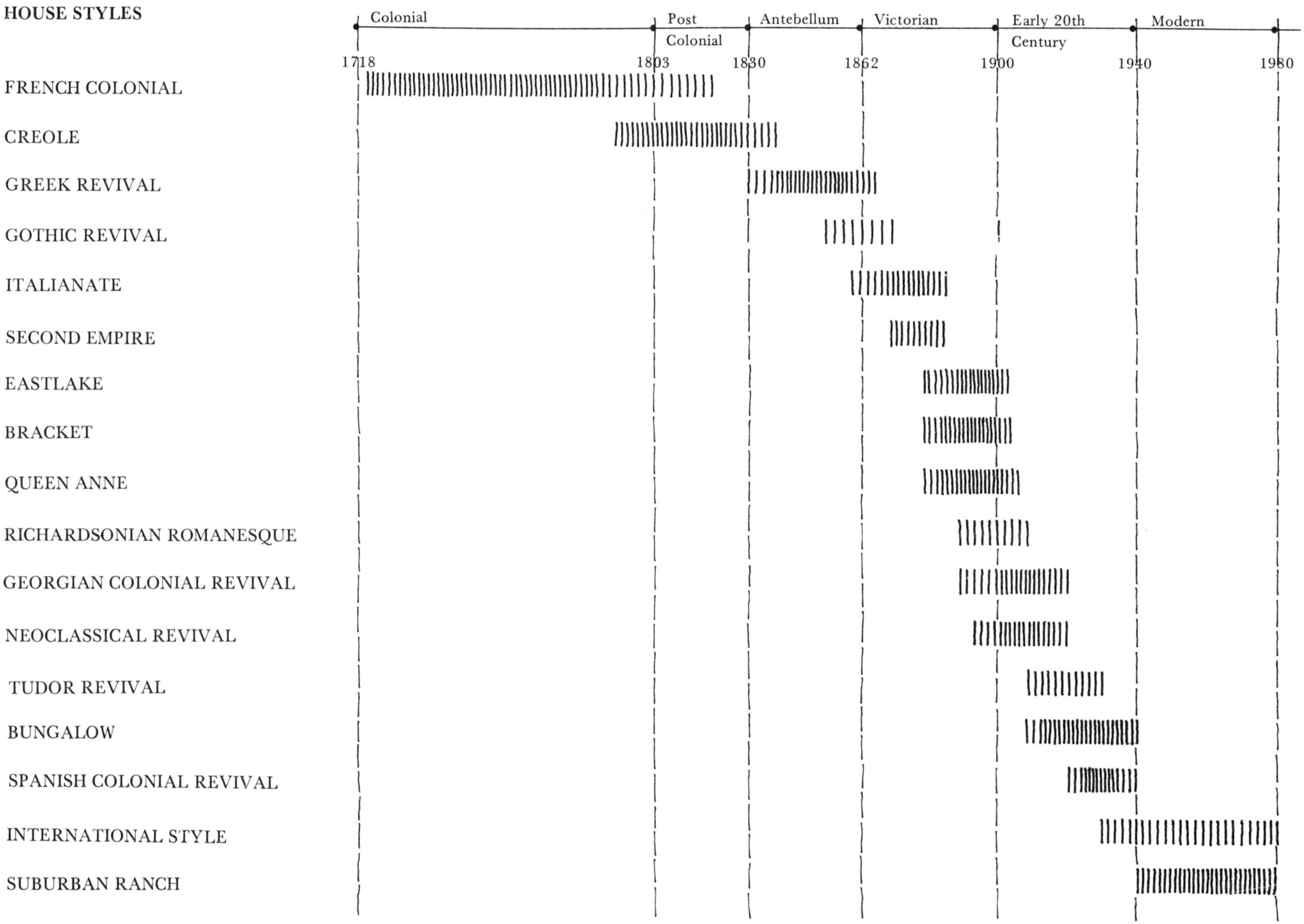

HOUSE STYLES

	Colonial	Post Colonial	Antebellum	Victorian	Early 20th Century	Modern

1718   1803   1830   1862   1900   1940   1980

FRENCH COLONIAL

CREOLE

GREEK REVIVAL

GOTHIC REVIVAL

ITALIANATE

SECOND EMPIRE

EASTLAKE

BRACKET

QUEEN ANNE

RICHARDSONIAN ROMANESQUE

GEORGIAN COLONIAL REVIVAL

NEOCLASSICAL REVIVAL

TUDOR REVIVAL

BUNGALOW

SPANISH COLONIAL REVIVAL

INTERNATIONAL STYLE

SUBURBAN RANCH

or fourteen, and when transoms over doors are included in the design they are rarely operable. Many of these replicas are constructed of "used bricks," intended to project a feeling of age, when in fact the historic structures of the city were built with new bricks that are now old. It is not uncommon to find that shutters fastened to the wall on these new structures are for ornamentation only; frequently they are of a size that would not cover the windows even if they were operable.

The location of a house can also aid in determining its authenticity. When the house-watcher happens upon a complex of 1830s Greek Revival townhouses in an 1890s Victorian neighborhood, he must seriously question the construction date of this discovery.

There is a great deal of joy awaiting anyone interested in exploring and understanding the residential landscape of New Orleans. An experienced house-watcher's ability to assess the characteristic nuances of the houses he passes and to sense the era in which they were constructed will greatly increase his appreciation of life in one of America's finest outdoor museums.

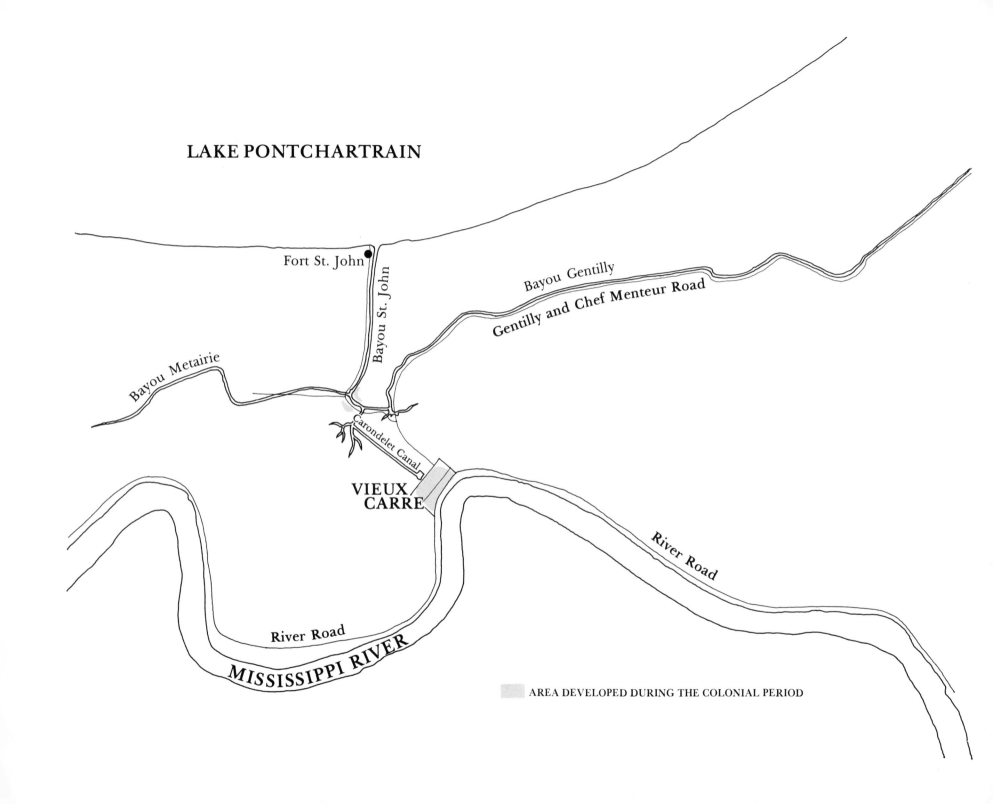

LAKE PONTCHARTRAIN

Fort St. John

Bayou St. John

Bayou Gentilly

Gentilly and Chef Menteur Road

Bayou Metairie

Carondelet Canal

VIEUX CARRE

River Road

River Road

MISSISSIPPI RIVER

AREA DEVELOPED DURING THE COLONIAL PERIOD

THE COLONIAL PERIOD (1718–1803)

In January 1699, French-Canadian explorer Pierre le Moyne, sieur d'Iberville, and his younger brother Jean Baptiste, sieur de Bienville, sailed into the Gulf of Mexico with four ships and approximately five hundred men on a mission for Louis XIV, king of France. They landed near present-day Biloxi, Mississippi, where they established a settlement, built a small fort (Fort Maurepas), and garrisoned it with eighty-one men.

After a short stay they continued westward, braving a gulf storm with high winds and driving rain. On March 2, 1699, they reached the Mississippi River by way of North Pass. Battling the strong current, the explorers ventured north up the mighty river.

On this expedition they were met by a group of Indians who led them to an Indian trading post situated in a crescent about one hundred miles above the river's gulf outlet. From this site they were led on a portage route to a village on a four-mile-long bayou, now known as Bayou St. John, which connected in turn with Lake Pontchartrain, Lake Borgne, and the Gulf of Mexico, providing a shortcut from the river to the open gulf.

After exploring the area the Frenchmen left without attempting to establish a settlement. However, their knowledge of the portage route and of the river crescent would later play an important role in the selection of the site of the city of New Orleans.

In the years that followed France became preoccupied with a losing war against England and exerted little effort to develop its Gulf Coast colonies at Biloxi and what is now Mobile, Alabama. When King Louis died in 1715, the country was nearly bankrupt.

A Scottish gambler named John Law arrived in France at about this time, maneuvered his way into French social circles, and intrigued the Duc d'Orleans with his plan for increasing the country's solvency by promoting a scheme to sell stock in the development of Louisiana. Soon French investors were purchasing stock in Law's Company of the West, later called the Company of the Indies.

In 1718 Bienville, who was now in charge of the Gulf Coast colonies (d'Iberville had died of yellow fever in Havana in 1706), was instructed by Law's company to establish a new colony on the lower Mississippi River. The colony was to be an economic venture rather than a military outpost like most French colonial settlements; it was intended to control the river and to serve as a trading post and administrative center for the company. Bienville returned to the river-crescent site he had visited nearly twenty years earlier and founded the city of Nouvelle Orleans, named, on the instructions of John Law, for Philippe, duc d'Orleans, regent for the young Louis XV.

Bienville landed a reluctant work crew of convicts and carpenters and began the task of cutting the dense vegetation that surrounded the chosen site. The first structures the colonists built were very basic and rather crude, patterned after the local Choctaw huts and constructed entirely of wood, which was readily available in the area. Many of these early houses, intended for use only until more permanent dwellings could be built, rotted, settled and cracked in the damp, soft soil, or were destroyed by the hurricanes that hit the city in 1719 and 1722. Within a few years construction methods improved as the settlers sought to build more permanent dwellings. The first brickyard was established about 1725, and brick foundations soon replaced the decaying wooden sills.

The new settlement was planned in a traditional French gridiron pattern by military engineer Pierre Leblond de la Tour in 1720, soon after he arrived in the French colony of Biloxi. The plan was symmetrical, with streets wrapped around a central square—Place d'Armes (now Jackson Square)—facing the river. A church was planned for the northern end of the square, with a prison, barracks, and a rectory nearby.

In 1721, with the population of New Orleans at 470, la Tour's assistant Adrien de Pauger arrived on the site and began the task of laying out the streets according to la Tour's instructions, utilizing the square as a focal point. The original plan called for the city to be enclosed by a fortification wall, with the area immediately outside the wall reserved for a commons—a designated open space where no construction was allowed. Thus, when the sites for the first plantations were granted, they were located beyond the limits of the commons.

The early years were far from easy for the French colonists. They encountered mosquitoes, mud, floods, hurricanes, soft soil, and hot, wet summers. They soon realized that the natural levee formed as the river deposited soil along its banks was not adequate as a barrier against flooding. In 1723 construction was started on the city's first man-made levee. The battle between New Orleans and the river had begun.

As the city grew, topographical conditions were the major determinants of the direction of expansion. Much of the area surrounding the established settlement consisted of swampland, with the only high ground running along the Mississippi River, Bayou St. John, and Bayou Metairie. These natural ridges, with their relatively firm soils, provided the only spines of land suitable for development. Since agriculture was the only viable economic endeavor, bit by bit land along these ridges—around Bayou St. John and the riverfront above and below the townsite—was cleared for plantations. The planters in these outlying areas soon began to build French Colonial plantation houses, which suited their way of life and responded to the environmental conditions they faced—the constant threat of flooding; the damp, soft soils; and the hot, humid summers.

In 1762 the French colony of Louisiana was ceded to Spain in a secret meeting between Louis XV of France and his first cousin, Charles III of Spain. France was glad to get rid of a losing investment, while Spain believed it was important to control the vast territory between her Floridian and Mexican holdings. In 1766 a Spanish governor arrived with ninety soldiers at the small village of 3,000 French-speaking colonists. But the transition from French to Spanish rule was not without turmoil, as the colonists were openly dissatisfied with the change in government. They rebelled against the new Spanish rule, forcing the governor to flee the city. King Charles responded by sending in the Irish-born general Alexander O'Reilly with an army of 2,600 soldiers. O'Reilly marched into the city to the sound of music and drums, imprisoned the leaders of the uprising, and promptly put an end to the French rebellion.

During the thirty-eight years of Spanish rule immigration laws were relaxed, allowing a greater number of people to settle in New Orleans. The Spanish governors brought many important changes to the colony, but the language and culture of the city remained primarily French. In 1782 the Spanish introduced the concept of the covered market, which soon replaced the French outdoor markets operating on the levee just above Place d'Armes. During the 1790s Governor Carondelet ordered the digging of the Carondelet Canal (later called the Old Basin Canal) and provided the city with its first streetlights, newspaper, theater, and policemen.

On March 21, 1788, the first of two great fires swept through New Orleans, destroying most of the Vieux Carre (French Quarter). Over eight hundred of the city's approximately eleven hundred buildings were burned, the majority of them simple wooden structures.

Six years later, on December 8, 1794, as the Vieux Carre was being rebuilt, a second great fire ravaged the city. Except for the Ursuline Convent built in 1745, no structures in the Vieux Carre remain intact from the French colonial era, although portions of French colonial structures were incorporated into the Cabildo and the Presbytere on Jackson Square when they were constructed after the fire of 1788. Soon after the second fire rigid building laws were passed, requiring that tile roofs be used on all buildings and that two-story buildings be constructed either of brick or *briqueté-entre-poteaux* (brick-between-post) and covered with cement stucco. Only one-story buildings with a maximum depth of thirty feet could be constructed entirely of wood.

Since the city was now under Spanish rule, most of the new construction was strongly influenced by Spanish design, for Spain had considerable experience with colonial building practices under subtropical conditions in Florida, the Caribbean, and Latin America. It was during this period that the Mediterranean ambience that still characterizes the French Quarter developed, with the introduction of two- and three-story stucco-covered brick townhouses with courtyards, arches, and wrought-iron railed balconies imported from Spain and Mexico. (Wrought iron was widely used for gallery railings, carriageway entrance gates, and fences until about 1850, when cast iron was introduced.) Many of these new houses were initially constructed with flat roofs used as outdoor patios, but because of severe leakage problems they were gradually covered by sloping roofs.

By the end of the eighteenth century the Creole (French-Spanish) culture was well established in New Orleans. In 1800, much to the joy of the French colonists, France regained control of the territory from Spain. But their joy was short-lived, for three years later the area was sold to the United States as part of the Louisiana Purchase, bringing an end to the colonial period in New Orleans.

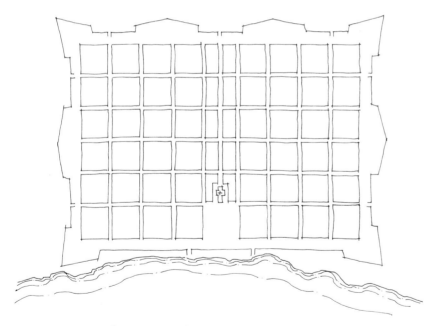

Plan of New Orleans (Vieux Carre), 1722

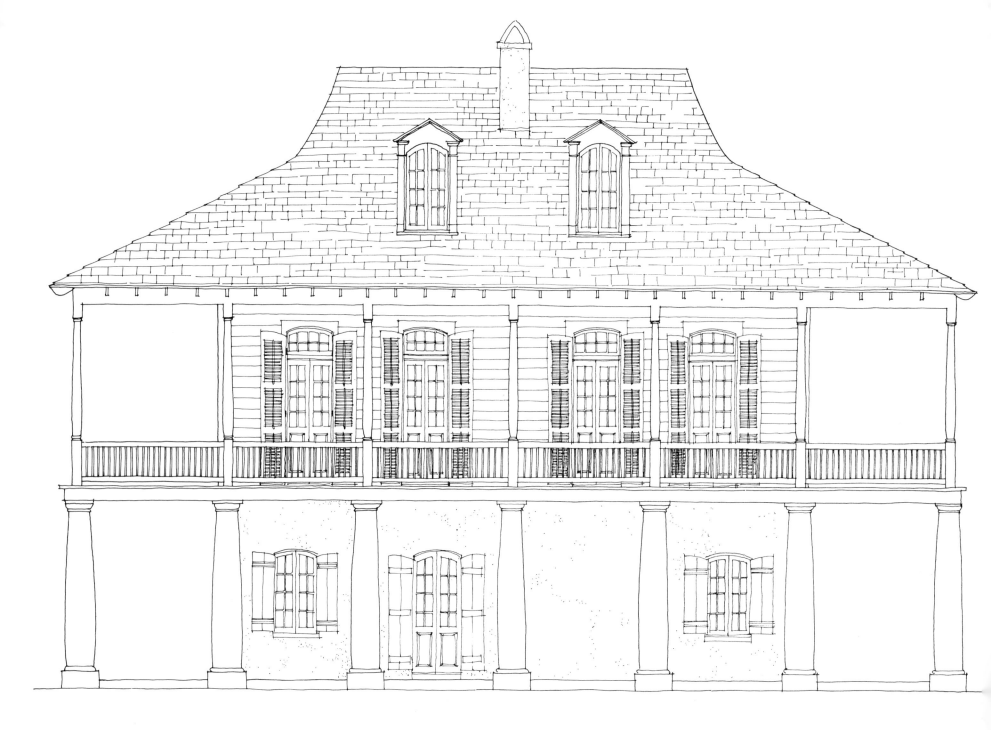

THE FRENCH COLONIAL STYLE (1720–1820)

French Colonial houses evolved from the very early temporary structures built by the first settlers to the huge raised homes of the wealthy planters.

The very early buildings were constructed of heavy timber framing—*colombage*—covered with wide horizontal boards. These dwellings were built on wooden sills placed directly on the ground. The roofs were steeply pitched, hipped, and covered with wood shingles or long strips of bark. The structures did not fare well in the soft soils and the wet, hurricane-prone climate.

When brick was introduced it was used as infill in the spaces between the heavy timber framework of the walls, a construction technique called *briqueté-entre-poteaux* that provided insulation against heat and cold and resulted in a more substantial structure than wood or bricks used alone. For a brief period, from about 1728 to 1730, the bricks were left exposed, creating a medieval-village effect. Since the local bricks were very soft and porous, this method soon proved impractical and the exterior walls were again covered with wood siding or cement stucco to keep out the moisture. A mixture of mud and moss was sometimes used as infill between the heavy timbers. This method was called *bousillage.*

Vertical-board shutters were used on windows and doors, and the more substantial buildings also had window sashes, which in most cases were covered with thin, semitransparent cloth pulled taut inside the frames.

Brick masonry walls were introduced in the 1730s in the two-story barrack buildings flanking the cathedral on opposite sides of the Place d'Armes. This building method proved unreliable, however; the barracks failed structurally and were demolished in the 1750s. Local builders concluded that because of the soft soil brick masonry was impractical in buildings of more than one story; from then on bricks were used in constructing the first story only, while *briqueté-entre-poteaux* covered with weatherboards or cement stucco was used for the second story.

Because of the hot, humid summers, houses were built with high ceilings, a practice that continued in New Orleans until the introduction of the Bungalow style in the early 1900s. The high ceilings allowed the hot air to rise while the heavier, cooler air settled, providing some relief from the scorching heat. Galleries were not constructed on the very earliest houses, but once their advantages in providing shade from the sun became apparent they became a standard feature of colonial architecture. The abundance of rainfall also contributed to their popularity, as they created exterior spaces protected from the rain and made it possible to keep windows open during wet periods to help circulate air.

During this period the planters outside the Vieux Carre developed the French colonial plantation house raised above the ground on massive columns supporting generous galleries. The ground level was used for storage, while the raised living area afforded protection from the damp soil and flooding and provided access to welcome summer breezes. Roofs were hipped and very steep, with a West Indies–style double pitch at the eaves extending over the galleries. Roof dormers with pilasters and arched or segmentally arched windows were common. Windows were the casement type with multiple lights and vertical-board shutters.

The architecture of the period reflected French and Spanish traditions as well as ideas imported from the Caribbean, where an early marriage of Indian and European cultures had given birth to picturesque houses that afforded good ventilation and ample shade.

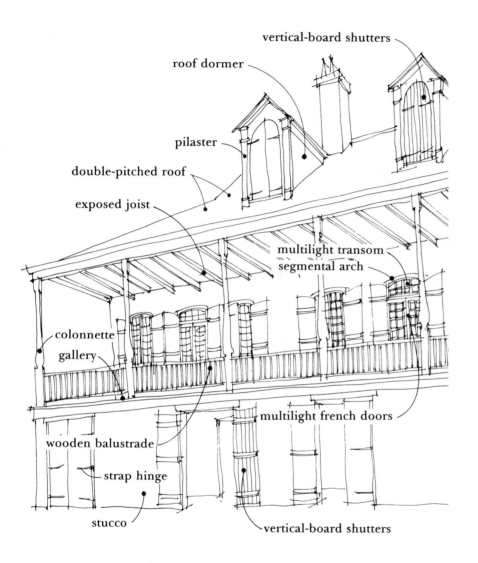

vertical-board shutters

roof dormer

pilaster

double-pitched roof

exposed joist

multilight transom
segmental arch

colonnette

gallery

multilight french doors

wooden balustrade

strap hinge

stucco

vertical-board shutters

FRENCH COLONIAL PLANTATION HOUSE

Madame John's Legacy, pictured here, was one of the first houses constructed in the Vieux Carre after the great fire of 1788. An urban adaptation of a French colonial plantation house, it is said to be a replica of the previous house on the same site, and is thus most likely typical of the urban houses of the period.

The walls of the first level are made of brick, stuccoed over, while the second level is *briqueté-entre-poteaux* covered with wide, beaded boards placed horizontally. The facade features a wide second-level gallery with delicate wooden balusters and slender colonnettes. The window and door surrounds are simple wood casings, with low segmental-arch heads, and all openings have vertical-board shutters with strap hinges. Two simply detailed roof dormers with casement windows are placed symmetrically in the double-pitched roof.

L. Vogt 82

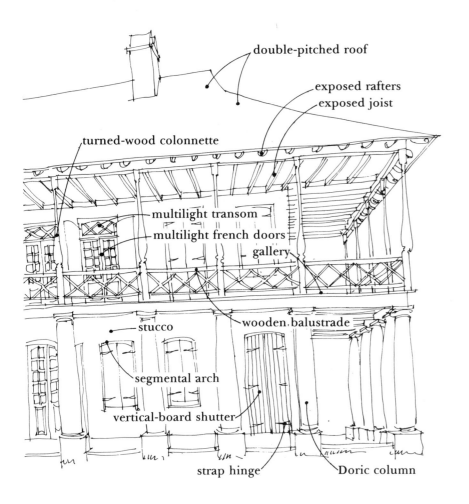

double-pitched roof

exposed rafters
exposed joist

turned-wood colonnette

multilight transom
multilight french doors
gallery

stucco

wooden balustrade

segmental arch

vertical-board shutter

strap hinge

Doric column

FRENCH COLONIAL PLANTATION HOUSE

The Pitot House on Bayou St. John, constructed in the late 1790s, is a fine example of a French colonial plantation house and one of the few remaining examples in the city. The house takes its name from one of the early owners, James Pitot, the first democratically elected mayor of the incorporated city of New Orleans.

Massive stucco-covered brick columns at the first level support a second-level gallery on the front and right side. An **X**-patterned wooden balustrade stretches between slender turned wooden colonnettes. Symmetrically placed chimneys pierce the ridge of a broad, double-pitched roof.

The house is constructed of *briqueté-entre-poteaux* covered with stucco. Each floor has three large rooms running the width of the building with two adjoining *cabinets* in the rear. Multilight casement windows and french doors with transoms are protected by vertical-board shutters with strap hinges. The windows and doors are topped with segmental-arch heads.

THE POSTCOLONIAL PERIOD (1803–1830)

For a number of years prior to the purchase of Louisiana by the United States, American frontiersmen had been journeying down the Mississippi River to New Orleans, bringing such cargoes as cornmeal, pickled pork, and whiskey. Frequently the Creoles purchased the Americans' keelboats after they arrived, dismantled them, and used the lumber for constructing houses, sidewalks, and wharves. The Creoles traded with the early frontiersmen, but they did not socialize with them.

Soon after the Louisiana Purchase Anglo-Americans began to pour into the city. The reputation of New Orleans as a city of opportunity prompted men of all classes, the cultured as well as the illiterate, to seek their fortunes in the cotton and river trades.

The Creoles, separated from the Americans by nationality, religion, customs, law, politics, and language, considered their civilization superior to that of the newcomers, many of whom they thought of as barbarians. They also resented the Americans' attitude that Louisiana was a conquered territory to be exploited for their personal benefit. The Anglo-Saxons, meanwhile, distrusted anyone who did not speak English. Both groups were determined to retain their cultural traditions and life-styles. Initially the upper classes of Creole society retained control of the economy of the city and much of its politics. But the number of Americans was increasing steadily, and a battle for supremacy became inevitable.

The early French colonists had planned a canal upriver of the Vieux Carre, immediately beyond the commons. Although the canal had not been constructed, it was still considered a good idea when the Americans took possession of the city in 1803. In 1807 Congress passed an act preserving a huge right-of-way for the proposed canal. The waterway was never constructed, but the creation of Canal Street provided an appropriate barrier between the Creole community in the Vieux Carre and the new American community to the west. This barrier became known as the "neutral ground," a phrase that has come to mean the median strip of a boulevard to New Orleanians.

The city's first waterworks was established in 1810. The system consisted of pipes made of hollow cypress logs into which river water was pumped by slave labor. The majority of the population, however, preferred water from private cisterns, which were generally located in the rear yard of each dwelling.

From its earliest years New Orleans had been known for its love of food and festivity. Most dining was in the home, but during the early 1800s the city's tradition of restaurant dining began. Creole men enjoyed leisurely meetings in cafes and bars, conducting business, arguing politics, and consuming coffee, liquor, and food.

In 1805 Bernard de Marigny, a Creole planter, subdivided his plantation immediately downriver from the Vieux Carre, creating the suburb of Faubourg Marigny. Its initial development consisted of simple Creole cottages inhabited by native-born artisans and workers, many of them "free persons of color." Significant development in Marigny began in the 1830s.

For the most part the Americans were unwelcome in the Creole faubourgs. After a failed attempt at buying land in Faubourg Marigny, they began to develop and build on the land above Canal Street in what was called Faubourg Ste. Marie (later changed to St. Mary). Originally subdivided by Don Beltran Gravier after the great fire of 1788, this "suburb" had been named in honor of Madame Gravier's patron saint. The first buildings constructed by the Americans, located in what is now the Central Business District, were primarily raised plantation houses on large tracts of land and cottages similar to those popular in the Vieux Carre at the time.

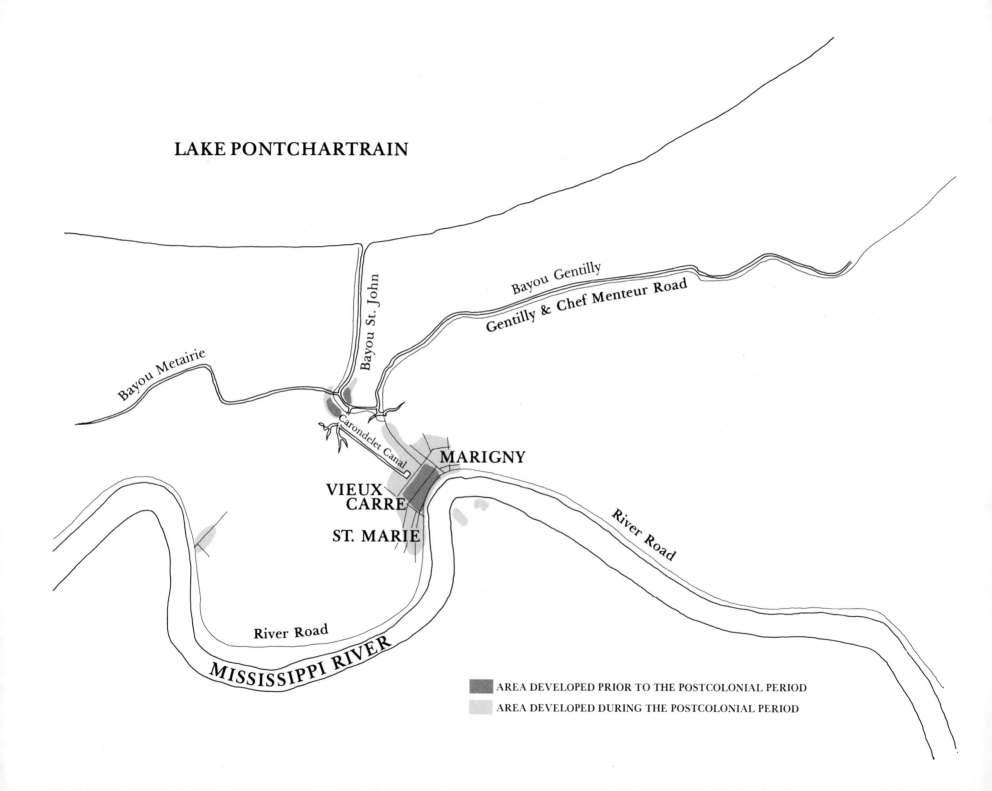

LAKE PONTCHARTRAIN

Bayou Gentilly

Gentilly & Chef Menteur Road

Bayou St. John

Bayou Metairie

Carondelet Canal

MARIGNY

VIEUX CARRE

ST. MARIE

River Road

River Road

MISSISSIPPI RIVER

■ AREA DEVELOPED PRIOR TO THE POSTCOLONIAL PERIOD

■ AREA DEVELOPED DURING THE POSTCOLONIAL PERIOD

Along with the influx of Americans into the city came a large number of French immigrants, refugees from revolutions in France and the West Indies. By 1810 the U.S. Census listed New Orleans, with a population of 17,224, as the fifth largest city in the United States behind New York, Philadelphia, Baltimore, and Boston.

By 1815 the population had reached 33,000, and the city was still growing rapidly. By 1820 it had increased to 41,000. Irish immigrants began arriving in the city during the 1820s, settling mostly in the vicinity of Tchoupitoulas Street in Faubourg St. Mary and Lafayette; this area became known as the Irish Channel.

The majority of the houses built during the postcolonial period were one-story Creole cottages and two- and three-story townhouses (Creole, entresol, and porte-cochere) with their associated outbuildings. From 1820 to 1835 there was a gradual shift from essentially Creole to essentially American building, influenced by house designs from the northeastern states. Soon new buildings in the Vieux Carre and the faubourgs were being constructed as row houses, with two to twelve identical houses attached to one another. Once introduced, the American townhouse, based on the English side-passage plan with an interior sidehall, gained acceptance rapidly. By 1830 even the Creoles were adopting the increasingly popular exposed red-brick designs, and slate was replacing tile and shingles as the most common roofing material. Around this time houses also began to take on classical Greek embellishments, ushering in the Greek Revival style that was to dominate New Orleans architecture for the next thirty years.

THE CREOLE STYLE (1790–1840)

The term *Creole* is used here to identify the style of buildings constructed in New Orleans by the Creoles from the late eighteenth century to the mid-nineteenth century. Their houses reflected both French and Spanish influence, tempered by the subtropical climate of the city. The major house types were Creole cottages and Creole, entresol, and porte-cochere townhouses.

The very early Creole cottages were constructed of heavy timbers, mortised and tenoned together, with brick infill (*briqueté-entre-poteaux*) stuccoed over for protection against moisture. Weatherboard siding and brick masonry with stucco were also commonly used. In the brick masonry cottages, the gabled side-wall usually extended a foot or two above the roof line, creating a protective fire barrier. Outbuildings, generally two stories high, were built in the backyards.

Some of the earliest Creole townhouses had stucco moldings around doors and windows, and stucco pilasters terminating at a stucco cornice. Most buildings with these features date from the late 1700s or early 1800s.

During the early 1800s the most popular method of construction was brick masonry covered with cement stucco, frequently painted pastel colors such as yellow, light green, pale blue, or apricot. During the 1820s, as the American influence spread in the city, townhouses were frequently constructed with exposed red-brick facades. Many houses of this period, built of the locally made porous brick, were painted red with the mortar joints painted white (these were known as "penciled" mortar joints). This technique was an attempt to solve the moisture problem inherent in the local bricks while retaining the appearance of exposed brick in the American style.

Creole-style townhouses generally had arched openings at the first level with multilight french doors and fanlight transoms behind iron bars. Openings on the upper levels of the earlier townhouses were french doors with multiple lights and panels below or casement windows. Soon after their introduction by the Americans around 1815, double-hung windows became very popular, eventually replacing casement windows as the most common type in the city. Most double-hung windows were six-over-six, six-over-nine, or six-over-twelve.

Shutters were used on all openings—usually the vertical-board type for greater security at the ground level and the operable-louver type on the upper levels to allow more light and ventilation. Balconies with wrought-iron railings were the general rule on multistory houses. The earlier wrought-iron designs were generally in a scroll or curve motif, while the later ones were simpler geometric patterns.

Roof dormers to allow light and ventilation into the attic space of houses were a common feature; there were usually two dormers on the front elevation and two on the rear. In most cases dormers had casement windows with segmental arches or round heads until about 1815, and six-over-six, double-hung windows thereafter.

During the 1830s and 1840s, as the Greek Revival movement gained momentum in New Orleans, many Creole houses took on such classical features as dentils and Greek key surrounds.

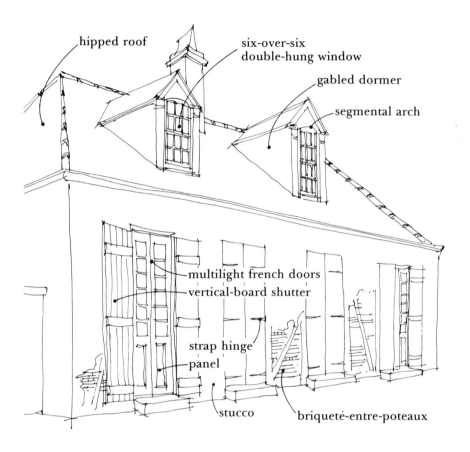

hipped roof

six-over-six
double-hung window

gabled dormer

segmental arch

multilight french doors
vertical-board shutter

strap hinge
panel

stucco

briqueté-entre-poteaux

CREOLE COTTAGE

A hipped-roof Creole cottage constructed very low to the ground and abutting the sidewalk. The facade openings are french doors with multilights above and panels below, with vertical-board shutters on strap hinges.

A pair of symmetrically placed, gabled dormers piercing the roof have six-over-six, double-hung windows with segmental-arch heads.

Construction is stucco-covered *briqueté-entre-poteaux,* visible in the areas where the stucco has peeled off.

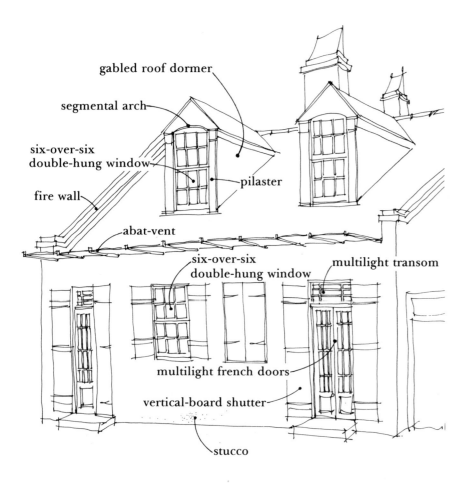

gabled roof dormer

segmental arch

six-over-six
double-hung window

fire wall

pilaster

abat-vent

six-over-six
double-hung window

multilight transom

multilight french doors

vertical-board shutter

stucco

CREOLE COTTAGE

This Creole cottage is an example of the *abat-vent* variety very common in the Vieux Carre. Fire walls project above the roof line at the side gables and the building is finished in smooth stucco.

The entrances have multilight french doors with multilight transoms. The windows are double-hung, six-over-six, and all openings except dormer windows have vertical-board shutters. The gabled roof dormers have segmentally arched, six-over-six, double-hung windows and flanking pilasters.

46

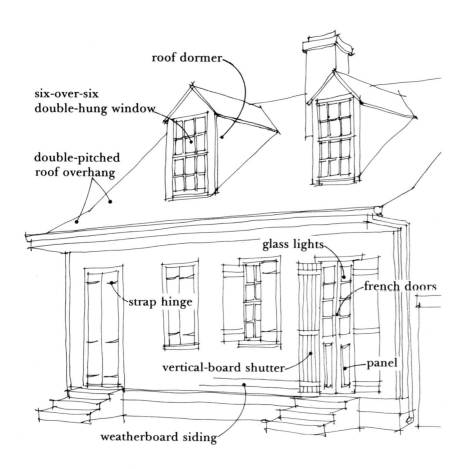

roof dormer

six-over-six
double-hung window

double-pitched
roof overhang

glass lights

strap hinge

french doors

vertical-board shutter

panel

weatherboard siding

CREOLE COTTAGE

This 1½-story Creole cottage with weatherboard siding has high side gables and a double-pitched front roof overhang. The four-bay front facade has french-door entrances with panels below and glass lights above. The two front-facade windows are double-hung, six-over-six. All first-level openings have vertical-board shutters with strap hinges.

The roof has a pair of gabled dormers with flat-headed, six-over-six, double-hung windows. The house sits directly on the sidewalk, raised only slightly above the ground.

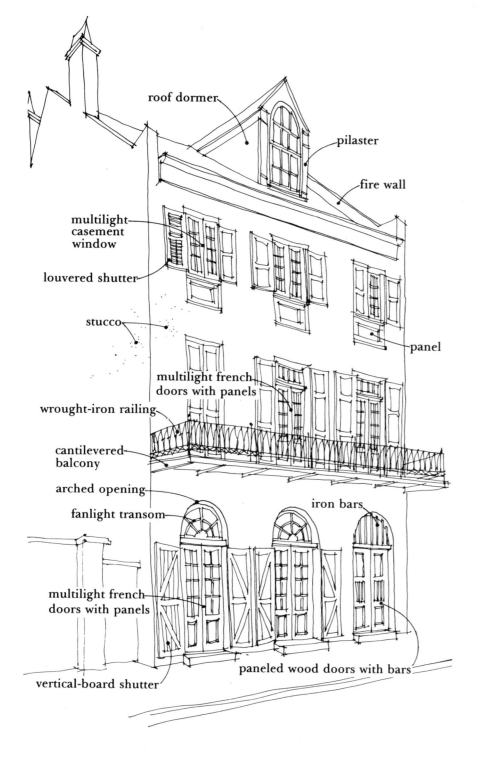

roof dormer

pilaster

fire wall

multilight casement window

louvered shutter

stucco

panel

multilight french doors with panels

wrought-iron railing

cantilevered balcony

arched opening

fanlight transom

iron bars

multilight french doors with panels

vertical-board shutter

paneled wood doors with bars

CREOLE TOWNHOUSE

A three-bay, three-story Creole townhouse with three arched openings with multilight french doors and fanlight transoms. The walls are of stucco-covered brick. A cantilevered balcony on the second level is enclosed by a delicate wrought-iron railing.

Multilight french doors with transoms above open onto the second-level balcony. There are multilight casement windows with a panel below each at the third level. Ground-level doors have vertical-board shutters for greater security, while second- and third-level openings employ full louvered shutters to increase light and ventilation.

Double chimneys extend from the side fire walls and a single dormer with a round-headed, multilight, double-hung window projects from the center of the roof.

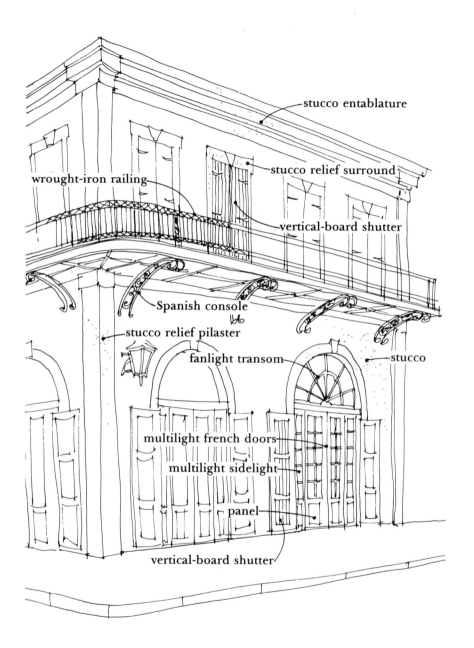

stucco entablature

stucco relief surround

wrought-iron railing

vertical-board shutter

Spanish console

stucco relief pilaster

fanlight transom

stucco

multilight french doors

multilight sidelight

panel

vertical-board shutter

CREOLE ENTRESOL TOWNHOUSE

The entresol townhouse is a building that appears to be two stories high when it is actually three. The first floor was used as a commercial establishment and the second as a storage floor for the business, while the third floor was the dwelling unit.

The openings at the first level of this house are french doors with multiple lights and wood panels, flanked by sidelights and topped with arched fanlight transoms. The second-story storage level is unperceived from the exterior; its floor is at the intersection of the french doors and the fanlight transoms, with the transoms serving as windows allowing light into the storage space. A balcony with wrought-iron railings supported by Spanish consoles wraps around two sides of this corner building at the third level. The stucco relief work forming corner pilasters, an entablature, and door surrounds is a characteristic that dates this building from the late 1700s or very early 1800s.

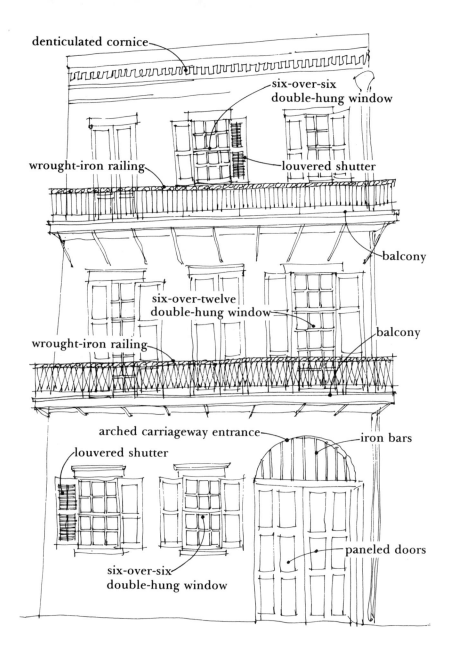

denticulated cornice

six-over-six
double-hung window

wrought-iron railing

louvered shutter

balcony

six-over-twelve
double-hung window

wrought-iron railing

balcony

arched carriageway entrance

iron bars

louvered shutter

paneled doors

six-over-six
double-hung window

CREOLE PORTE-COCHERE TOWNHOUSE

The prominent feature of this three-story brick townhouse is a large arched carriageway entrance with iron bars above its double doors. Such carriageways were generally paved with brick or flagstone and led into the rear courtyard.

While many houses of this type had commercial shops on the ground floor, this particular example was strictly residential. (Buildings with commercial establishments normally had glass french doors at the ground level in addition to the carriageway entrance, whereas this house has only windows.) Wrought-iron railings, a common feature of Creole townhouses, enclose narrow balconies at the second and third levels. Louvered shutters are used on all openings except the carriageway. The exposed red-brick facade and the dentilwork in the cornice reflect the American influence that was common from the 1820s on.

Porte-cochere houses were constructed throughout the Vieux Carre. Although many of their features have been altered through the years, many carriageway entrances are still intact, offering passersby interesting views of rear outbuildings and secluded courtyards. These courtyards, with their fountains and tropical foliage, have brought joy to many a pedestrian who, browsing through the streets of the French Quarter, has caught a momentary glimpse into the past.

L. Vogt 80'

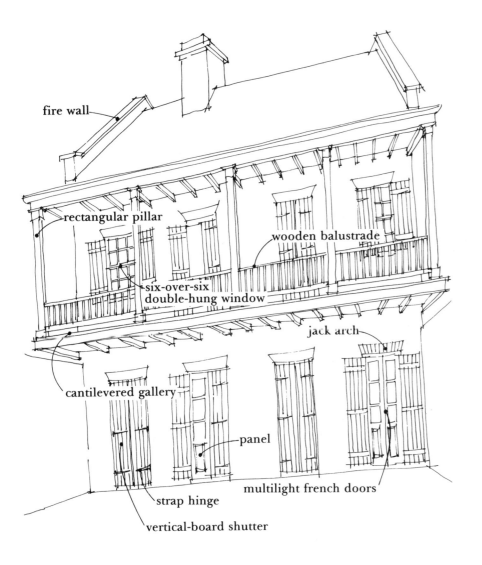

fire wall

rectangular pillar

wooden balustrade

six-over-six
double-hung window

jack arch

cantilevered gallery

panel

multilight french doors

strap hinge

vertical-board shutter

CREOLE OUTBUILDING

A typical two-story outbuilding, commonly found throughout the Vieux Carre and in surrounding areas. This four-bay brick structure has vertical-board shutters with strap hinges over glass-light french doors at the ground level and a combination of french doors and six-over-six windows at the second level. A jack arch provides the structural support over each opening.

The cantilevered gallery at the second level has a wooden balustrade with delicate square balusters and five simple, rectangular wooden pillars supporting the roof extension above. A brick fire wall extends above the roof at each side, separating the building from identical neighboring structures. Brick walls enclose the flagstone-paved courtyard between the outbuilding and the main house.

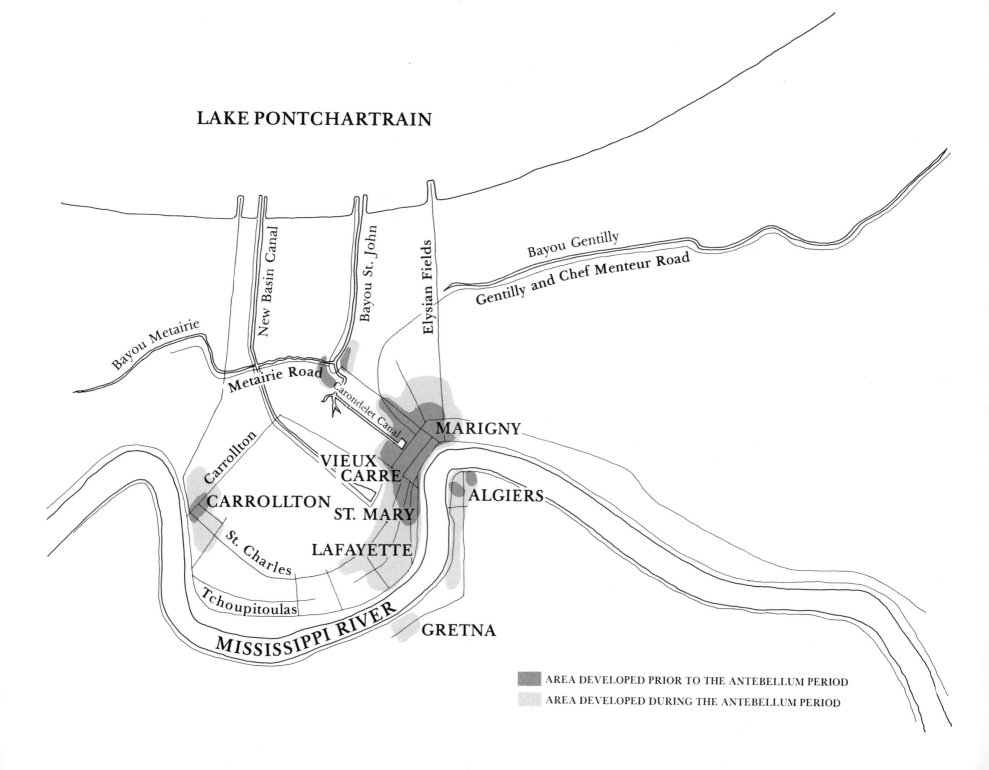

LAKE PONTCHARTRAIN

Bayou Gentilly

Gentilly and Chef Menteur Road

Bayou Metairie

New Basin Canal

Bayou St. John

Elysian Fields

Metairie Road

Carondelet Canal

MARIGNY

Carrollton

VIEUX
CARRE

CARROLLTON

ST. MARY

ALGIERS

St. Charles

LAFAYETTE

Tchoupitoulas

MISSISSIPPI RIVER

GRETNA

AREA DEVELOPED PRIOR TO THE ANTEBELLUM PERIOD

AREA DEVELOPED DURING THE ANTEBELLUM PERIOD

THE ANTEBELLUM PERIOD (1830–1862)

The period between 1830 and 1862 was the most glamorous and prosperous in the city's rich history. New Orleans hosted wealthy cotton and sugarcane planters, fancy riverboats, and sailing ships from all over the world. Immigrants were arriving every day, and new buildings were being constructed throughout the city, which now boasted fine restaurants, grand hotels, a flourishing opera, and festivities including lavish balls, banquets, and parades. New Orleans was the wealthiest city in the United States. Gambling and dueling were common, as was the practice of voodoo.

However, the glamour and prosperity coexisted with the miseries of urban life. Much of the city was filthy, its many unpaved streets frequently flooded by heavy rains. Its sewers were open drains. Typhoid, cholera, malaria, and yellow fever plagued residents, who struggled through twelve devastating epidemics in thirty-five years. The citizens of New Orleans would not drink the river water, preferring their own backyard cisterns, which unbeknownst to them were the breeding grounds for the Aedes aegypti mosquito, carrier of the deadly yellow fever. In 1853 more than 7,800 New Orleanians died of the dread disease. The death rate in the city was twice that of most urban areas.

As the American population in New Orleans increased, its cultural and political influence grew. While the Creoles retained their stronghold in the Vieux Carre, the Americans continued to build above Canal Street in Faubourg St. Mary. They built Lafayette Square, hoping to outshine the Creoles' Place d'Armes (renamed Jackson Square in 1851 to honor General Andrew Jackson, who saved the city from the British at the Battle of New Orleans in 1815). In 1832, realizing the need for a direct, navigable water route connecting Lake Pontchartrain to the American sector, they formed a company for the digging of a new canal. The New Basin Canal was 6½ miles long and took six years to build. Many lives were lost during its construction, as laborers died of sunstroke, malaria, cholera, and yellow fever.

The Americans were very successful businessmen and an increasing political force in the city, but for some time the Creole majority on the city council prevented such improvements as street paving and wharf construction in the American sector. Around 1835 antagonism between the two cultures reached its peak; soon the struggle for economic supremacy shifted in favor of the Americans. In 1836 they flexed their new political muscles by petitioning the state legislature to create separate entities within the city. As a result of this petition New Orleans was divided into three distinct municipalities: the Vieux Carre (the Creole sector), Faubourg St. Mary (the American sector above Canal Street), and Faubourg Marigny (downriver from the Vieux Carre). This tripart system eventually proved unworkable, however, and in 1853 the city was reunited.

During the antebellum period land in the Vieux Carre became very scarce, forcing the wealthy Creoles to look elsewhere for new homesites. They did not want to cross Canal Street into the American sector; nor did they wish to build in Faubourg Marigny, which was inhabited primarily by craftsmen, farmers, and free persons of color. The Creoles therefore chose to build to the north along the Esplanade Ridge, the closest high land available. The stately homes they constructed along Esplanade Avenue rivaled those being built by the wealthy American merchants and planters on large lots on the Livaudais Plantation above the river. (This area—now known as the Garden District—was incorporated in 1833 as Lafayette City and annexed by the city of New Orleans in 1853.)

Meanwhile the steady influx of German and Irish immigrants—recruited to dig canals, improve streets, and build railroads—required housing. To fill this need, American entrepreneurs constructed inexpensive Creole cottages and wood-frame double-gallery houses, mostly along the river in the Irish Channel.

In 1840 the Duverje Plantation (Algiers Point), originally a land grant from King Louis XIV of France to Bienville, was subdivided and quickly began to develop as a separate community.

New Orleans continued to grow rapidly; by 1840, with a population of 102,193, it had surpassed Philadelphia and Boston to become the third largest city in the United States after New York and Baltimore, and second only to New York as a port. Cotton, the chief crop of southern planters, was shipped through the port on steamboats. Eventually cotton presses constructed on the riverfront became a vital aspect of the booming port economy.

Until the mid-1820s New Orleans had enjoyed a monopoly on trade between the Northeast and the Midwest. In 1825 the Erie Canal was completed, opening up a new transportation route between these two regions. Many merchants now found it cheaper to ship cargo to the Northeast through this new canal than by way of the Mississippi River and the sea. But this was only the beginning of potential trouble for New Orleans, as new canals were being planned and the first railroads were about to begin operation.

When the railroads reached Chicago and St. Louis, New Orleans no longer enjoyed a monopoly on cargo transportation in the Mississippi Valley. Within a short period of time both railway cities had surpassed the southern port in population. As these new transportation centers were established in the northern states, it became obvious that if the South were going to compete it too would need railroads. The new industry was soon developing in New Orleans.

Two successful local railway systems opened in the city during this period: the Pontchartrain and the New Orleans and Carroll-ton Railroad. The Pontchartrain ran from the Mississippi River levee at Elysian Fields to the lake, a distance of approximately five miles. The majority of its passengers were New Orleanians on outings to the lakefront and passengers from ships arriving at or departing from New Orleans by way of Lake Pontchartrain.

The New Orleans and Carrollton Railroad, which staged its maiden trip on September 26, 1834, served as the catalyst for growth "uptown." It ran from the downtown business district on Canal Street, along St. Charles Avenue through Lafayette City, to the tiny resort town of Carrollton. This same route, which has been traveled by double-decker mule cars, steam engines, and electric engines (the present cars date from the 1930s) is still being used by the St. Charles Avenue streetcar.

By 1840 Louisiana had forty railroads, although some existed only on paper. The industry was growing fast, but it was ill-conceived and uncoordinated; nearly all of the companies ended in bankruptcy.

By the late 1830s American townhouses dominated Faubourg St. Mary. Row houses were rapidly evolving into the Greek Revival style common at the time in New York, Philadelphia, and Baltimore. The sidehall, English-style plan gradually became more popular than the Creole townhouse, porte-cochere, and entresol house types.

During this time gray granite pilasters were introduced as an architectural feature on the ground level of buildings in the Vieux Carre and Faubourg St. Mary. Many buildings previously constructed with arched brick openings at street level were modernized, with these rectangular granite pilasters replacing the original arches. This change provided more windows for ground-floor shops, and allowed more natural light to reach the interiors. The major streets of the city were now being lit at night by gas lanterns suspended on ropes, while the less important streets were lit with oil.

As growth continued, Greek Revival became even more popular, dominating residential design throughout the city. The culture in which it flourished was founded on a love of classical myth, classical literature, and classical art. It was a highly aesthetic culture, eagerly searching for an American expression. Five-bay American cottages, raised cottages, American townhouses, and double-gallery houses were common. The shotgun house which began to appear during this period soon became one of the most common house types in the city, retaining its popularity for approximately one hundred years.

During the 1840s water- and steam-powered sawmills and nail-making plants were being established throughout the country, bringing about a revolution in the design of houses. The common heavy-timber frame structures being constructed at this time required skilled workmen with special tools and were time-consuming to build. The balloon frame, said to have been originated in Chicago by George W. Snow, surveyor and civil engineer, used lightweight "dimensional" lumber, mostly two-by-four and two-by-six inches. With this construction method a house could be easily put together by any careful workman capable of sawing to a line and driving a nail. Skeptics, doubting their structural stability, prophesied that a strong wind would send such houses flying through the air like balloons—hence the term *balloon frame.* However, the light wooden frames proved practical, rapidly replacing heavy-timber frame construction as the most common method of building. This new technique allowed much greater design freedom, a freedom that eventually blossomed in the Victorian period.

At about the same time the practice of building houses on piers became popular. By raising his house slightly (usually about three feet), a homeowner could avoid problems with insects, chronic dampness, and torrential downpours, and allow ventilation under the house. This method of construction remained popular until the advent of the Suburban Ranch style after World War II.

Cast iron was probably introduced in New Orleans in 1849, with the construction of the Pontalba Buildings flanking Jackson Square. Designed by James Gallier and later modified by Henry Howard, the buildings utilized cast iron extensively, and it soon gained enormous popularity, primarily in the Vieux Carre and to some extent in Faubourg St. Mary. In many instances cast-iron columns, galleries, balconies, and railings were added to existing structures, substantially changing their appearance—and the character of the streets. Caution should always be exercised in trying to determine the construction date of a building utilizing cast-iron ornamentation; these buildings are best understood when one learns to peer through the lace of ironwork and see what stylistic characteristics lie beyond.

By mid-century Americans were beginning to question the intellectual and cultural basis of the classical tradition and a growing protest against revivalism began to emerge. Americans were starting to concentrate on the present, no longer feeling the need to emulate the past, and a new generation was turning its attention to the pursuit of wealth. The emergence of the new rich, combined with this emphasis on the present, would eventually strike a fatal blow to the concepts of Greek Revivalism, for if these newly acquired riches were to be fully enjoyed, they had to be made obvious to all; ostentation was becoming a new ideal in residential design. Around 1850 two Gothic-style houses were constructed in the city, anticipating by ten or fifteen years the beginning of the Victorian era in New Orleans architecture.

By 1860 New Orleans was the largest cotton market in the world with port trade totaling $324 million and wharf tonnage double that of New York City. Louisiana's per-capita wealth was second only to Connecticut's. New Orleans was an international melting pot, with a population gleaned from thirty-two nations. Forty-one percent of its residents were foreign-born.

Trouble between the North and the South had been brewing for some time, and in January 1861 the Louisiana legislature voted to secede from the Union, following South Carolina, Mississippi, Alabama, and Florida. On March 25 Louisiana joined the Confederate States of America: New Orleans was the largest and richest city in the newly formed Confederacy.

In April 1861 the Civil War began. New Orleans—protected by Fort Jackson and Fort St. Philip on the Mississippi River approximately seventy-five miles below the city—seemed secure. But in March 1862 a Union fleet of warships and mortar boats engaged the forts in battle. After five days and nights of artillery bombardment, the Union fleet managed to maneuver past the Confederate barricade, and, after overcoming a Confederate defense fleet, continued upriver, arriving in New Orleans on April 25.

Six days later General Benjamin Butler strode into New Orleans, destined to become one of the most hated men in the city's history. His heavy-handed rule was reinforced by 18,000 troops, an army of occupation that would rule the city for the next fifteen years. The occupation by Federal troops, the abolition of slavery, the chaos of the Reconstruction era, and the loss of river trade brought to an end the flamboyant life of antebellum New Orleans.

THE GREEK REVIVAL
(1830–1865)

The Greek Revival style first began to appear in New Orleans about 1830. It was the fourth phase—after Georgian, Federal, and Jeffersonian Classicism—in the evolution of classical revival architecture in America. However, except for a few Federal-style buildings, it was the first to exert a strong influence in New Orleans since the previous three phases had developed on the Eastern Seaboard during a period when New Orleans was a French and Spanish colony, unaffected by the architecture favored in the English colonies.

The style, which draws its inspiration from the architecture of ancient Greece, was launched in 1818 with the design of the Second Bank of Philadelphia, the result of a competition won by William Strickland, a former pupil of British architect Benjamin Henry Latrobe. (Latrobe had migrated to the United States in 1796 and in 1798 designed the Bank of Pennsylvania, the first American building to incorporate a classical Greek order.) America, still in its youth and searching for meaning, was striving to be the Athens of the New World. The Greek tradition symbolized liberty, and the style quickly spread throughout the country.

New York architect Minard Lafever is generally considered a major force in the popularization of the Greek Revival style. His first three books, *The Young Builder's General Instructor* (1829), *The Modern Builders' Guide* (1833), and *The Beauties of Modern Architecture* (1835), were widely used by practicing architects throughout the country. In 1835 two other New Yorkers, James Gallier and Charles B. Dakin, arrived in New Orleans, established an architectural practice, and helped spread the philosophy of the style through their execution of numerous buildings in the city.

As the Americans continued to pour into New Orleans from the Eastern Seaboard, they brought with them their architectural ideals. The sidehall American townhouse, with its red-brick facade, classical Greek detailing, white trim, and green shutters, was the standard house for the newcomers. These buildings were very similar in appearance to those being constructed in New York, Philadelphia, and Baltimore at the time. However, in response to the subtropical climate, the New Orleans houses were built with higher ceilings than their northern counterparts.

Greek Revival houses were characterized by simplicity, strength, and dignity. The local Greek Revival architects were more interested in emulating Greek architecture to solve the design problems of a growing community than in copying Greek temples. Thus, for the most part, the basic house forms of the style in New Orleans were not Greek temple forms, but rather the common house types of the period—American townhouses as well as cottages, raised cottages, and double-gallery homes—embellished with Greek details.

One of the major trademarks of Greek Revival is the Greek-key doorway (also known as crossettes), characterized by a slightly overlapping lintel and a slight flaring out of the face of the surround from the top to the bottom. Other distinguishing features of the style are a low-pitched roof, full entablature supported by Greek columns, and such Greek ornamentation as dentils, egg-and-dart molding, rosettes, palmettes, honeysuckles, and acanthus leaves.

Entrance doors were generally paneled, frequently flanked by sidelights and a rectangular transom, and framed with classical pilasters and cornice. Window surrounds were simple and severe, and shutters were most often the operable-louver type. Door and window openings were always flat-topped, as ancient Greek structures did not use arches.

There are five classical orders—three Greek (Doric, Ionic, and Corinthian) and two Latin (Tuscan and Composite). The Greeks had a number of varieties of each order, and these were further

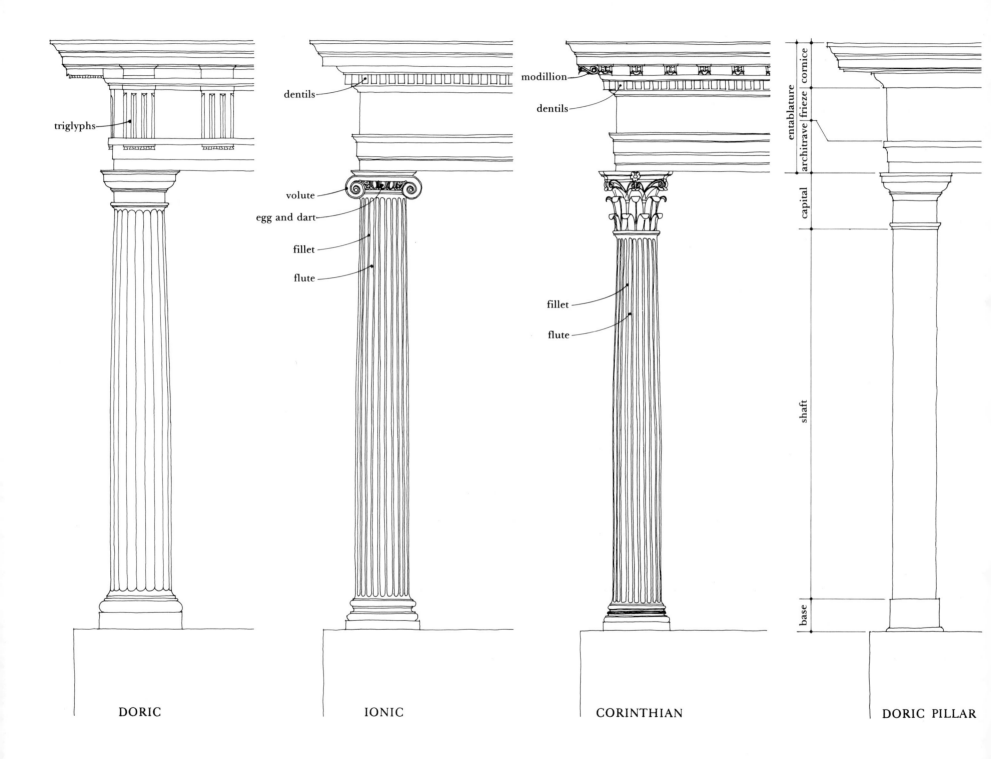

triglyphs

DORIC

dentils

volute
egg and dart
fillet
flute

IONIC

modillion
dentils

fillet
flute

CORINTHIAN

cornice
frieze
architrave
entablature

capital

shaft

base

DORIC PILLAR

manipulated during the revival periods to accord with American taste, often at the whim of the carpenters constructing a particular house. The result was a free, rather than strict, interpretation of the ancient prototypes. One common modification was the omission of fluting from the Doric column; another was the use of square or rectangular pillars in lieu of round columns.

In New Orleans the most frequently used of the three Greek orders were Doric and Ionic; in the majority of cases the more ornate Corinthian order was not utilized until the Italianate style became popular.

Prior to the 1850s brick American townhouses normally had simple wrought-iron railings, influenced by the Creole buildings in the Vieux Carre, while wooden Greek Revival houses had balustrades composed of simple, square wooden balusters. After their introduction in 1849 cast-iron railings became very common, especially in the Vieux Carre.

Greek temple, Athens, c. 430 B.C.

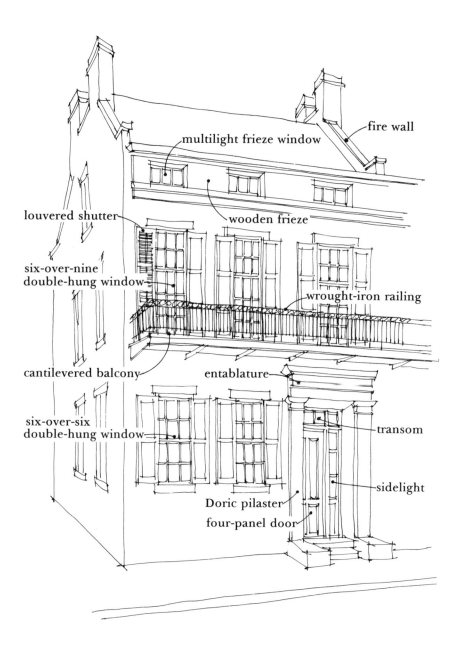

multilight frieze window

fire wall

louvered shutter

wooden frieze

six-over-nine
double-hung window

wrought-iron railing

cantilevered balcony

entablature

six-over-six
double-hung window

transom

sidelight

Doric pilaster

four-panel door

GREEK REVIVAL AMERICAN TOWNHOUSE (ROW HOUSE)

This 2½-story brick row house is typical of the type and style popularized in New Orleans during the 1830s and 1840s. The three-bay facade features a four-panel door with sidelights and a rectangular transom recessed behind an entranceway composed of wooden Doric pilasters and a heavy entablature—a distinguishing feature of the American townhouse.

A wrought-iron railed balcony is cantilevered from the second level. Windows on the first level are six-over-six; the full-length windows on the second level are six-over-nine, while window openings in the wooden frieze are divided into three parts. Full louvered shutters are employed on all window openings. A brick fire wall extends above the roof, separating the house from its attached and identical neighbor.

L. vogt 80

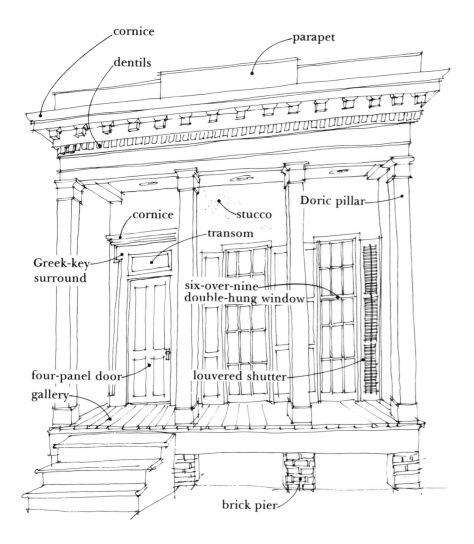

cornice

dentils

parapet

cornice

stucco

transom

Doric pillar

Greek-key
surround

six-over-nine
double-hung window

four-panel door

gallery

louvered shutter

brick pier

GREEK REVIVAL
SHOTGUN SINGLE

This three-bay wood-frame Greek Revival shotgun single on brick piers has a four-panel door with rectangular transom and a Greek-key surround, capped with a simply detailed cornice. The full-length, six-over-nine, double-hung windows open onto a front gallery and have full louvered shutters and very simple casings.

Four rectangular Doric pillars support a well-detailed entablature articulated with modillions, dentils, and a low parapet. The front facade is finished in smooth stucco while the sides and rear are probably covered with weatherboard siding. A low-pitched hip roof is completely concealed by the entablature and parapet.

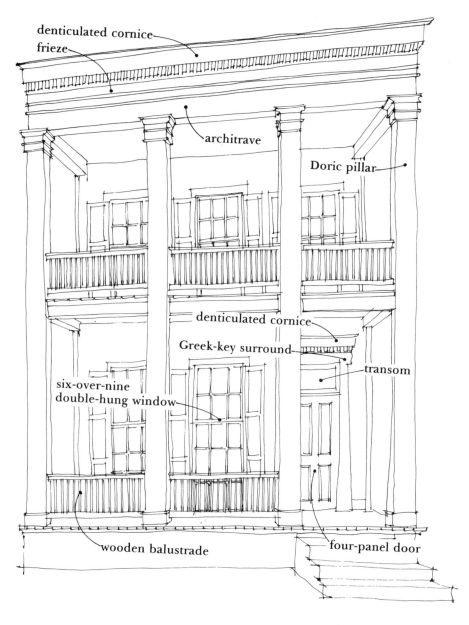

denticulated cornice
frieze
architrave
Doric pillar
denticulated cornice
Greek-key surround
transom
six-over-nine
double-hung window
wooden balustrade
four-panel door

GREEK REVIVAL DOUBLE-GALLERY HOUSE

A two-story, wood-frame Greek Revival sidehall house on brick piers with full-length Doric pillars supporting the upper gallery and the entablature. The entrance features a Greek-key motif and denticulated cornice around a four-panel door and transom.

The full-length windows are six-over-nine, with simple casings and full louvered shutters. The entablature, with denticulated cornice, is simple and restrained.

The delicate square wood balusters on this house were popular in Greek Revival construction in New Orleans until the early 1850s, when cast iron became readily available and very popular.

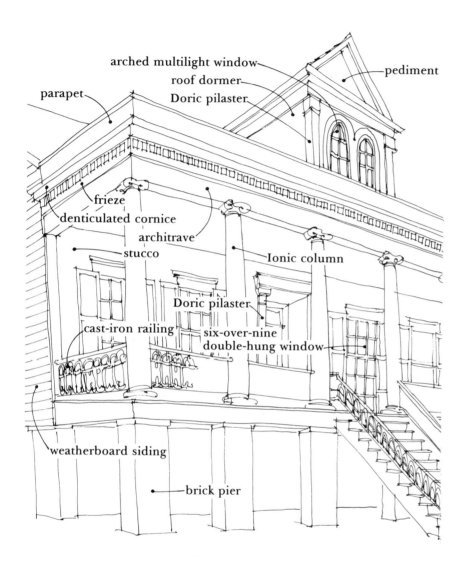

arched multilight window
roof dormer
Doric pilaster
pediment
parapet
frieze
denticulated cornice
architrave
stucco
Ionic column
Doric pilaster
cast-iron railing
six-over-nine
double-hung window
weatherboard siding
brick pier

GREEK REVIVAL RAISED AMERICAN COTTAGE

A wood-frame Greek Revival raised American cottage with weatherboard siding on the sides and rear, and smooth stucco on the front. A spacious front gallery with a cast-iron railing is supported by massive brick piers, while the entablature with denticulated cornice is supported by six Ionic columns. A large pedimented roof dormer with double arched openings (these openings are influenced by classical Roman architecture, since the Greeks did not utilize the arch) is situated above the five-bay, center-hall structure. The recessed doorway is embellished with pilasters and an entablature.

The full-length windows in the front facade are double-hung, six-over-nine, while all other windows are six-over-six. All windows employ full louvered shutters. A wide wooden stairway with cast-iron railings is centered in the facade.

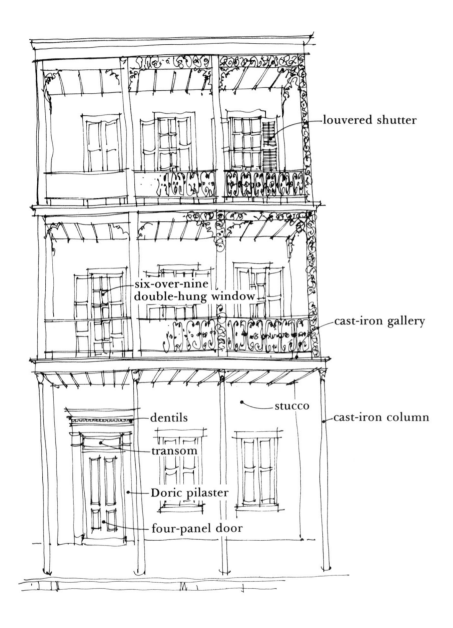

louvered shutter

six-over-nine
double-hung window

cast-iron gallery

dentils

stucco

cast-iron column

transom

Doric pilaster

four-panel door

GREEK REVIVAL
AMERICAN TOWNHOUSE

A Greek Revival three-bay, three-story, stuccoed brick residence with a deep cast-iron gallery on the second and third levels extending over the sidewalk and supported by delicate cast-iron columns below.

The doorway, with a four-panel door and rectangular transom, is recessed behind an entrance composed of a denticulated entablature and wooden Doric pilasters.

The full-length windows on the upper levels are double-hung, six-over-nine. All windows have very simple unadorned surrounds and full louvered shutters. Cast-iron galleries like the one illustrated here were frequently added to older Creole-style houses and were also common during the Italianate period. The style of this house is not determined by the cast iron, which is a Victorian inspiration, but rather by the building behind it.

THE VICTORIAN PERIOD (1862–1900)

During the 1850s the Victorian aesthetic—first evident in the Gothic Revivalist movement of the 1840s—began to sweep the country. Its tenets included variety, texture, playfulness, and a general distaste for classicism.

The Victorian period in New Orleans is generally divided into two subperiods—High Victorian (1862–1880), during which Italianate and Second Empire were the prevalent house styles, and Late Victorian (1880–1900), with Eastlake, Bracket, Queen Anne, and Richardsonian Romanesque styles dominating residential architecture. In New Orleans the most popular house types of the period were five-bay American cottages, shotguns, camelbacks, and double-gallery houses. For the most part the transition to the Victorian aesthetic in New Orleans was evolutionary rather than revolutionary: in the late 1850s new houses being constructed in the Greek Revival style gradually began incorporating Italianate detailing and ornamentation, evolving into the highly ornate Italianate houses of the 1860s and 1870s.

New Orleans felt the consequences of the Civil War, but its economy was not nearly as affected as that of most of the South. Soon after the war ended in 1865 activity began to revive. In an effort to stimulate economic trade, political leaders rebuilt much of the city's port facilities. Construction activity, which had come to a virtual standstill during the war, also began to increase.

The war had contributed to the eclipse of New Orleans in population by a number of cities, primarily by speeding the industrialization of the North and by further stimulating the construction of northern railroads. These railroads did not replace the river as a transportation route, but they did help bring about its decline; the railroads were fierce competitors for the transportation of goods that had to reach their destination in a hurry, but the river still commanded the bulk-cargo commerce, where delivery time was not a serious problem. The northern railroads now carried most of the general cargo from the Midwest to the East, while the heavier bulk cargo, most of which was coal from Kentucky and Illinois and grain from the upper Midwest, continued to travel down the Mississippi through New Orleans. In addition the cotton trade with Europe and New England expanded, increasing shipments from five million bales a year in the best prewar years to ten million a year by the late 1890s. And a new agricultural trade was developing with Latin America, primarily because of the city's strategic location at the interface of the Gulf of Mexico and the Mississippi River.

As was the case in much of the South, extensive railroad systems were somewhat delayed in coming to New Orleans. In the 1870s the Deep South rail system was begun with New Orleans as its center. Within a short time the city had succeeded in becoming the country's main rail outlet to the Gulf of Mexico. When the system was completed, New Orleans had six major lines reaching into the interior of the continent to Cincinnati, Chicago, Kansas City, and Los Angeles.

During the late 1860s and 1870s development continued upriver along the railway line on St. Charles Avenue, slowly closing the gap between the urbanized area of New Orleans and the town of Carrollton, which had developed where St. Charles Avenue now meets Carrollton Avenue. Carrollton was incorporated into the city in 1874. Development was also gradually spreading out on both sides of the Esplanade Ridge and downriver beyond Faubourg Marigny. By 1878 the population had reached 210,000.

Irish and German immigrants continued to arrive in New Orleans, and they were now joined by Italians. The Italians gravitated to the French Quarter—most of the Creoles had left the Quarter and moved to the nearby faubourgs—occupying

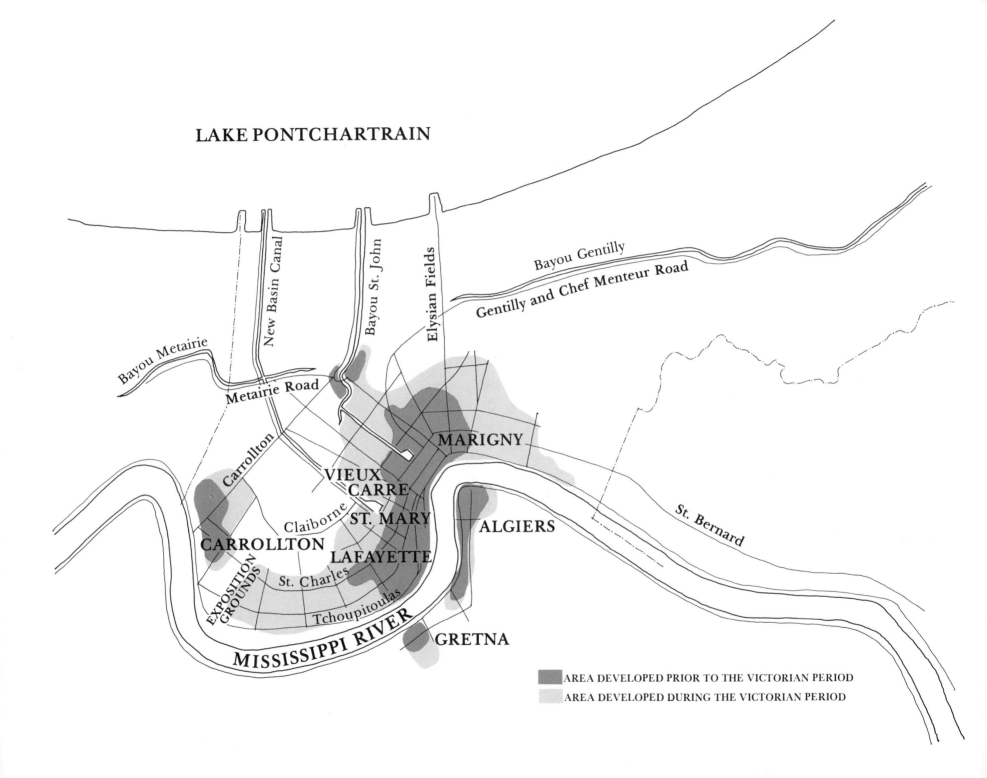

LAKE PONTCHARTRAIN

New Basin Canal

Bayou St. John

Elysian Fields

Bayou Metairie

Bayou Gentilly

Gentilly and Chef Menteur Road

Metairie Road

Carrollton

MARIGNY

VIEUX CARRE

St. Bernard

Claiborne

ST. MARY

CARROLLTON

LAFAYETTE

ALGIERS

EXPOSITION GROUNDS

St. Charles

Tchoupitoulas

GRETNA

MISSISSIPPI RIVER

AREA DEVELOPED PRIOR TO THE VICTORIAN PERIOD
AREA DEVELOPED DURING THE VICTORIAN PERIOD

the deteriorating older structures. The fact that the buildings remained occupied prevented many from being demolished.

New Orleans had always been a crowded city by southern standards, partly because of European building traditions and partly because of the limited buildable high land. As the influx of immigrants continued, land became more and more scarce. Pressures of growth had been partially relieved by ferry service that had made the West Bank accessible, but the options for expansion remained very limited. The shotgun house type, ideally suited for long narrow lots, was a natural for these conditions. Consequently thousands of shotgun houses, mostly four-bay doubles, were constructed on lots generally 30 feet wide by 120 feet deep.

During the last two decades of the nineteenth century Victorian taste exhibited an even greater desire for complexity, and variation in texture and ornament was utilized wherever opportunity allowed. Sawmills were cutting timber into dimensional lumber, and the lathe and jigsaw were rapidly turning out mass-produced ornamentation—turned columns, brackets, balusters, and scrollwork. Ornamental millwork was readily available from catalogues published by companies such as Roberts & Co., Proprietors of the Louisiana Steam Sash, Blind and Door Factory. Its popularity grew rapidly.

By now the Greek Revival austerity so highly revered during the antebellum period had vanished completely. Turned-wood elements such as columns, balusters, and friezework spindles and a wide variety of jigsaw work were extensively utilized. It was an age of playful colors and elaborate ornamentation. The majority of the houses constructed were wood frame on brick piers, with weatherboard siding or wood shingles, or a combination of both. (One exception to this rule was the Richardsonian Romanesque style, with its massive, rough-stone facades, although such buildings were not nearly as common as Queen Anne, Bracket, and Eastlake houses.) In the Vieux Carre a number of structures were demolished and replaced by Eastlake- and Bracket-style single and double shotguns and camelbacks.

The 1884 World's Fair and Cotton Centennial Exposition announced to the world that New Orleans was once again open for business. The fair had to be located on a large tract of land, relatively high, with easy access by public transportation. Only one area met these criteria: a tract lying between the urban center of the city (the Vieux Carre and Faubourg St. Mary) and the recently annexed suburb of Carrollton, and conveniently pierced by the New Orleans and Carrollton Railroad.

The Exposition was a yearlong extravaganza, attracting hundreds of thousands of visitors. It is doubtful whether it had any effect on increasing cotton sales, and it showed a loss financially, but it left a lasting imprint on the city. When it was over the land between the river and the railway line on St. Charles Avenue was turned into Audubon Park and the land on the lake side was preserved for Tulane and Loyola universities.

With the tensions of Reconstruction gone, the city was experiencing steady growth. The population had increased from 168,674 in 1860 to 287,104 in 1900. The urbanized area extended upriver all the way to Carrollton, with development spread in a crescent from the river four or five blocks beyond St. Charles Avenue. Downriver the urbanized sector extended from the Mississippi approximately to St. Claude Avenue, and along Esplanade Avenue to Bayou St. John. Scattered development was also taking place northward toward the lake, but it remained sparse since high land was scarce.

By the turn of the century newly constructed, classically inspired houses painted all white were being enthusiastically received and it was obvious that the Victorian period was coming to an end. It had been an era that borrowed little from the past, a period that created its own aesthetic, unlike any other in American history.

THE GOTHIC REVIVAL (1850–1870)

The Gothic Revival style was instrumental in ushering in the Victorian era in America. Although not very common in New Orleans, it was extremely popular in some parts of the country, with examples ranging from picturesque cottages to magnificent churches. However, its major characteristic, the pointed arch, does appear on various buildings and houses in the city.

The style takes its inspiration from the Gothic cathedrals of Europe, built from the twelfth to the fifteenth centuries. The choir of the Abbey Church in St. Denis near Paris, France, constructed from 1140 to 1144, is generally considered the first Gothic building. The abbey combined the pointed arch, buttresses, and ribbed vaulting in a system of technical and aesthetic unity; although each of these elements had been created at an earlier date (the pointed arch, for example, appears to have its origin in seventh-century Egypt), they had never before been utilized together.

One of the most influential voices in the shift from classical to romantic ideals in America was that of Andrew Jackson Downing (1815–1852). A successful landscape architect in New York, Downing published a series of books that greatly affected the tastes of mid-nineteenth-century America.

Downing's *The Architecture of Country Houses,* aimed at American readers, was a somewhat simplified and condensed version of J. C. Loudon's *Encyclopaedia of Cottage, Farm, and Villa Architecture and Furniture,* published in London seventeen years earlier. In his book Downing set forth his philosophy of the ideal American way of life and the houses in which to fulfill that ideal, professing the superiority of Gothic Revival over the reigning Greek Revival. Downing also relied heavily on the ideas and works of other architects such as Alexander Davis, who designed in a variety of styles but showed a preference for the Gothic Revival.

The Gothic Revivalists painted houses in natural colors— shades of reddish brown, gray, and rose. In their attempt to establish harmony with nature, they used landscaping extensively. Also characteristic of the style are steeply pitched gable roofs with highly ornate bargeboards. Gothic arched windows frequently had diamond-patterned lights and operable louvered shutters with matching pointed arches. Hood molds over windows were also very common. New Orleans Gothic Revival houses were usually built of either wood frame with weatherboard siding, exposed brick, or stuccoed brick. The houses were generally rather delicate in appearance. The first Gothic Revival houses in New Orleans were constructed around 1850.

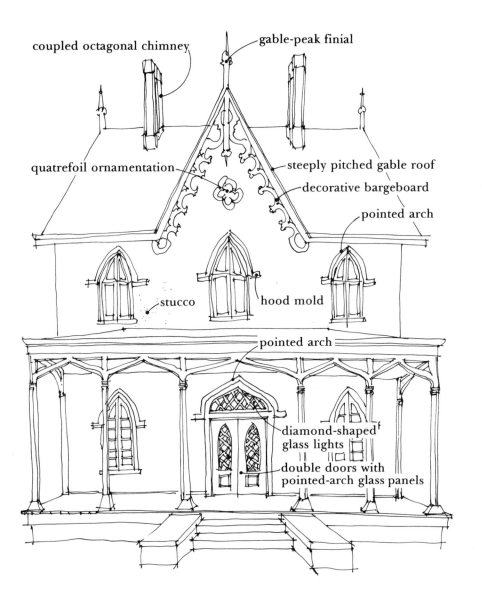

coupled octagonal chimney

gable-peak finial

quatrefoil ornamentation

steeply pitched gable roof

decorative bargeboard

pointed arch

stucco

hood mold

pointed arch

diamond-shaped glass lights

double doors with pointed-arch glass panels

GOTHIC REVIVAL HOUSE

The pointed arches on this house immediately identify it as Gothic Revival. Other features common to the style include steeply pitched gable roofs with decorative bargeboards, quatrefoil ornamentation, and gable-peak finials.

The windows and doors have Gothic arches and hood molds. The double front doors and transom feature diamond-shaped glass lights. The front facade is symmetrical and the walls are finished in smooth stucco. A pair of tall, coupled, octagonal brick chimneys rise from the center roof ridge.

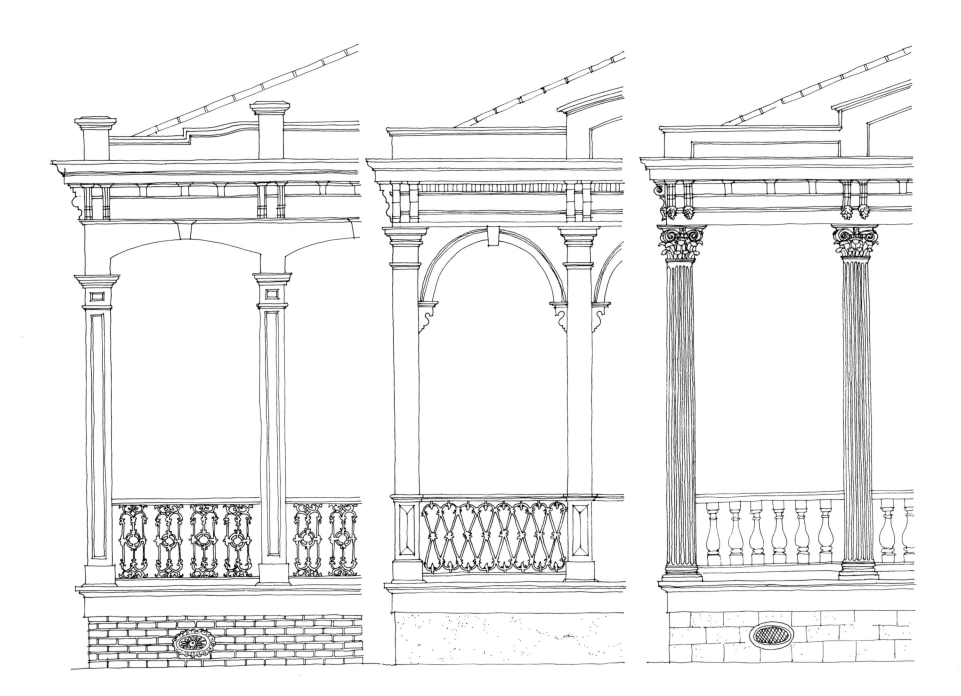

THE ITALIANATE STYLE (1860–1885)

In the late 1850s Greek Revival architecture in New Orleans began to take on a more ornate character, and within a decade it had evolved into the Italianate style, which dominated the city's residential architecture throughout the 1860s and 1870s.

The Victorian period had introduced to the city such new design features as vibrant colors and beveled and stained glass. Columns (normally fluted) evolved from Doric and Ionic to the more ornate Corinthian order. It was quite common to find columns of the Ionic order on the first level of a double-gallery house and Corinthian on the second.

The Italianate style was inspired by Italian Renaissance architecture and the rural architecture of northern Italy and introduced to America by way of England. Some of its major characteristics are bracketed cornices with paired brackets in the entablature aligned over columns, segmental arches, stilted arches, a pronounced arch keystone, quoins, rustication, and decorative parapets. Dormers, found most often on Italianate raised cottages, were frequently enhanced with decorative volutes on each side, while rectangular pillars and pilasters were sometimes embellished with wood molding, producing a layered, paneled look. A semioctagonal room (usually a dining room) projecting on one side of the house was also a common feature.

Roofs were low and inconspicuous, similar to those of Greek Revival houses, and windows were double-hung, usually two-over-two, or full-length two-over-four, with operable louvered shutters. Windows and doors frequently terminated with segmental-arch heads. The building types were still primarily those of the antebellum period—raised American cottages, shotguns, camelbacks, and double gallery houses.

By 1880 Italianate houses had begun to incorporate newly popular Eastlake and Queen Anne ornamentation, resulting in the Bracket style.

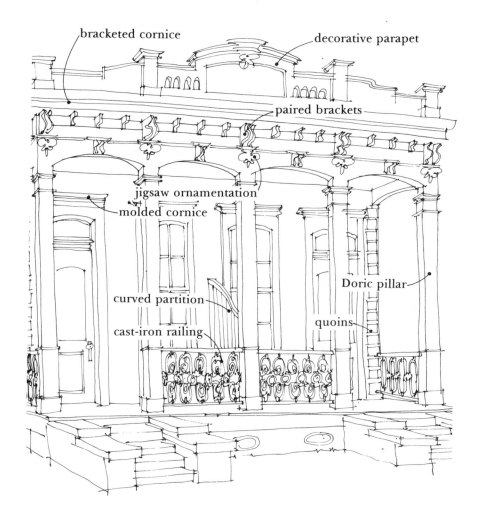

bracketed cornice

decorative parapet

paired brackets

jigsaw ornamentation

molded cornice

Doric pillar

curved partition

quoins

cast-iron railing

ITALIANATE CAMELBACK

This Italianate double camelback features a decorative entablature and parapet supported by rectangular Doric pillars. The construction is wood frame with drop siding on the front facade and weatherboard siding on the sides and rear. The house is raised approximately three feet on brick piers.

The segmentally arched openings of the gallery are repeated in the windows and door transoms on the front facade. A low, curved partition separates the two dwellings. The doorways and the six-over-nine, full-length, double-hung windows are capped with molded cornices. Quoins are applied to corners of the front facade. A cast-iron railing encloses the gallery.

The entablature features a bracketed cornice with jigsaw ornamentation and paired brackets aligned over the pillars. The parapet is very visible and highly ornate, completely hiding the low-pitched roof.

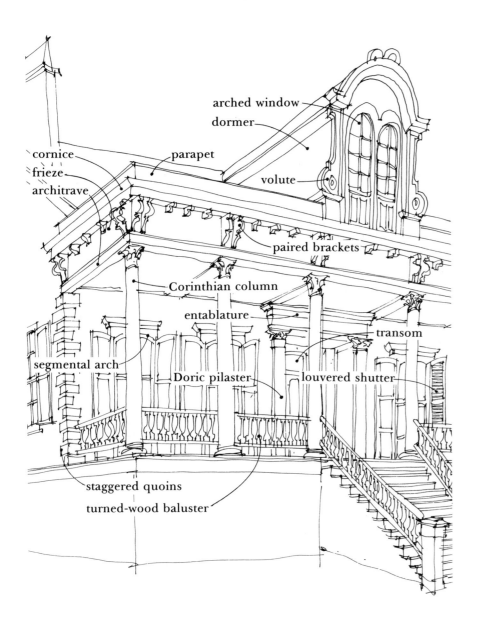

arched window

dormer

cornice
frieze
architrave

parapet

volute

paired brackets

Corinthian column

entablature

transom

segmental arch

Doric pilaster

louvered shutter

staggered quoins

turned-wood baluster

ITALIANATE RAISED AMERICAN COTTAGE

This large, five-bay, center-hall raised cottage has weatherboard siding on the rear and sides and drop siding on the front—a treatment commonly used for a decorative effect.

The recessed entrance features a beveled-glass door with a transom above and an entablature supported by Doric pilasters. Windows have segmental-arch tops and full louvered shutters.

Six fluted Corinthian columns support an entablature with a bracketed cornice; paired brackets are centered above the columns. A large central dormer with paired arched windows and volutes rises from a simple, low parapet.

Staggered quoins wrap around the corners of the front facade. The gallery balusters are of the ornamental turned-wood type. A semioctagonal bay with a bracketed cornice and four-over-four, double-hung windows projects from the side elevation.

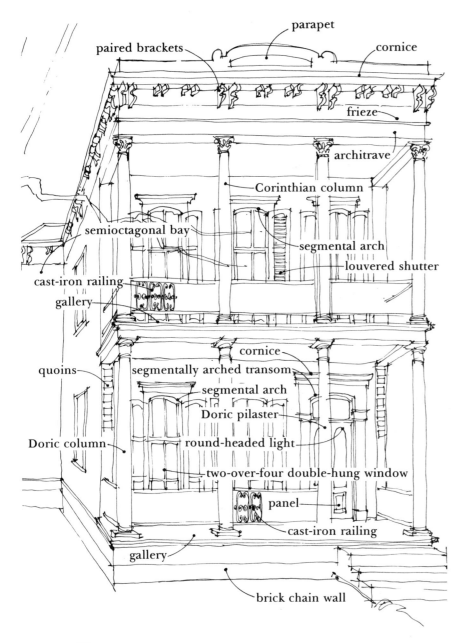

parapet

paired brackets

cornice

frieze

architrave

Corinthian column

semioctagonal bay

segmental arch

louvered shutter

cast-iron railing

gallery

cornice

quoins

segmentally arched transom

segmental arch

Doric pilaster

Doric column

round-headed light

two-over-four double-hung window

panel

cast-iron railing

gallery

brick chain wall

90

ITALIANATE SIDEHALL DOUBLE-GALLERY HOUSE

This two-story, wood-frame structure on a brick chain wall has fluted Doric columns at the first level and fluted Corinthian columns at the second. (When Italianate houses have two different orders of columns, the more ornate columns will usually be found at the upper level.) Ornamental cast-iron railings embellish the spacious gallery.

The paneled entrance door has double, round-headed lights and a segmentally arched transom above. The entranceway surround consists of pilasters supporting a segmental arch and cornice. Segmentally arched, double-hung, full-length windows are two-over-four, with full louvered shutters.

The elaborate entablature features a cornice with paired brackets aligned over the columns and a decorative parapet. Corner quoins ease the transition from weatherboard siding on the side elevations to drop siding on the front facade. A two-story semioctagonal bay is terminated by a bracketed cornice that extends completely around the house.

THE SECOND EMPIRE STYLE (1870–1885)

The term *Second Empire* refers to the period of Napoleon III's reign in France, from 1852 to 1870. It was during this time that Paris underwent a major rebuilding program that transformed it into a city of grand boulevards and buildings of monumental character. One of the first great public works of the period, and one of Napoleon's most famous projects, was the enlargement of the Palace of the Louvre in 1857. Known as the New Louvre, the extension was visually heavier and more sculptural than the seventeenth-century original.

Two of the first major nondomestic American buildings in the style, both designed by James Renwick, were the Corcoran Gallery begun in 1859 in Washington, D.C., and the Main Hall of Vassar College near Poughkeepsie, New York (1860). The State, War, and Navy Building (1871–1888) in Washington, designed by Alfred B. Mullett, and the Philadelphia City Hall (1871), designed by John McArthur Jr., were two of the largest and grandest Second Empire buildings in the U.S. Since the style enjoyed its greatest popularity during General Grant's presidency it is sometimes referred to as the General Grant style.

The trademark of the style is the mansard roof, originated by the French architect François Mansart (1598–1664) and reintroduced and popularized throughout Europe and the United States during the Second Empire. (It is generally accepted that the word *mansard* is derived from the architect's name, although it is also possible that it comes from the French word *mansard* ["attic"]). The roof consists of a double slope, the lower very steep, the upper somewhat flatter. This roof form incorporates a living space in what is, in essence, an attic. Although the concept was quite successful in France and the northern U.S., in the New Orleans climate the attic space was very uncomfortable throughout the summer months because of the intense heat.

Any house with a mansard roof can generally be classified as Second Empire. Most of the detailing and ornamentation was Italianate, including quoins, segmentally arched windows and doors, a bracketed cornice at the roof line, and classical columns. Bull's-eye dormers piercing the roof are common and unique to this style. A tower housing a stairway was frequently a major feature.

Most of the Second Empire houses in New Orleans are very large, expressing a strong sense of monumentality.

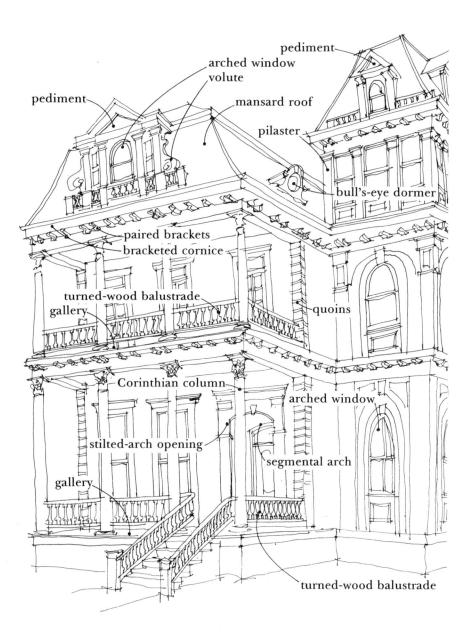

pediment

arched window
volute

pediment

mansard roof

pilaster

bull's-eye dormer

paired brackets
bracketed cornice

turned-wood balustrade
gallery

quoins

Corinthian column

arched window

stilted-arch opening

segmental arch

gallery

turned-wood balustrade

SECOND EMPIRE
DOUBLE-GALLERY HOUSE

This Second Empire house has a double gallery with a turned-wood balustrade on the front facade. Corinthian columns support the massive mansard roof, the distinguishing characteristic of the style. Bracketed cornices at the first and second levels—with paired brackets over the columns—encircle the house.

The entrance is recessed behind a stilted-arch opening with pilasters and cornice; the glass-light door has a transom above. Full-length, double-hung windows opening onto the galleries have molded casings and decorative cornices. A highly ornate dormer with an arched window features a classical pediment and pilasters, volutes, and a turned-wood ornamental balustrade. A single bull's-eye dormer pierces the side roof.

A tower with a mansard roof, dormers, and a bracketed cornice projects from the side elevation and houses a monumental stairway. A combination of weatherboard and drop siding is used throughout, with quoins or pilasters on most corners.

94

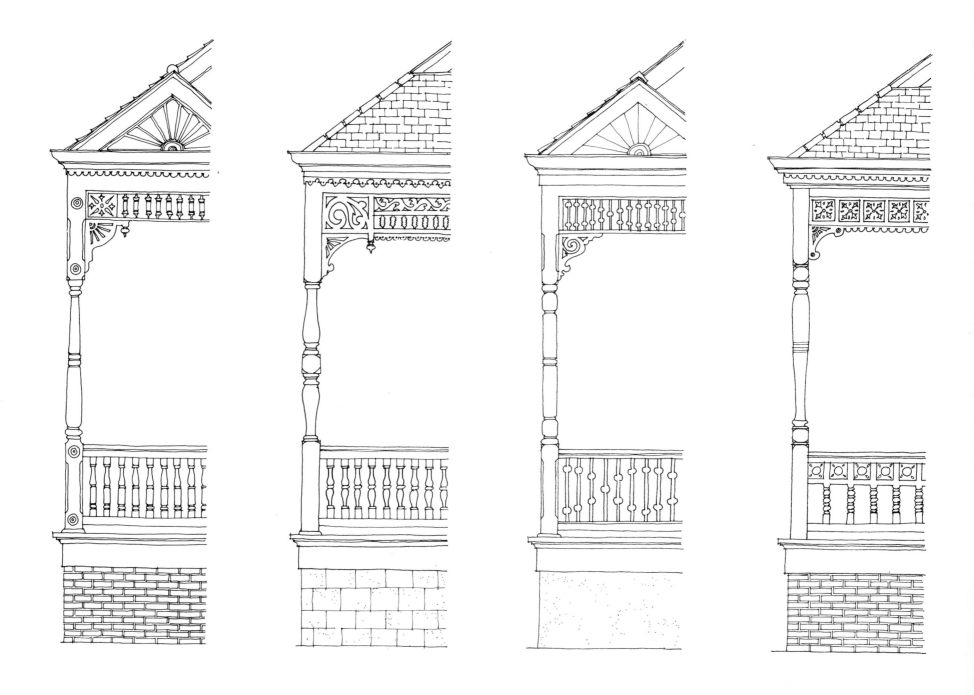

THE EASTLAKE STYLE (1880–1905)

In 1868 an English architect named Charles Locke Eastlake, son of the painter Sir Charles Eastlake, wrote *Hints on Household Taste.* In 1872 the first American edition appeared in Boston. It was an immediate success, with six more editions issued during the next eleven years. This book on furniture design provided the ground rules for what became known in America as the Eastlake style. Although flattered by the popularity his books had attained in America, its author had little sympathy for the application of his ideas to the design of architectural millwork, the results of which he considered extravagant and bizarre. He openly expressed regret that his name was associated with the style.

This style, with its turned columns and balusters in the shape of table and chair legs, characterizes a large number of houses built in the city during the Late Victorian period. Many of the picturesque shotguns lining New Orleans streets are in the Eastlake style.

Porches and galleries were numerous and generous, embellished with brackets, piercework, and spindle bands. Bargeboards were frequently decorated with jigsaw appliqué. The highly textured and very quaint appearance of Eastlake houses is commonly referred to as "Victorian," although "Victorian" actually refers to a period that included many different styles, one of which was Eastlake.

Glasswork—stained, etched, and beveled—was also an important Eastlake feature. The more expensive houses used leaded stained glass, while common builders' houses featured stained glass in wood frames on doors and gable windows. Front-facade windows opening onto galleries were likely to be full-length, double-hung, two-over-four. Occasionally stained glass was used in the upper sashes of these windows.

Most Eastlake houses were of wood-frame construction on piers, with weatherboard siding. Drop siding on the front facade and corner quoins were common. Wooden porch balustrades consisted of ornate turned balusters. The most common house types associated with the style were shotgun singles and doubles, double-gallery houses, and camelbacks.

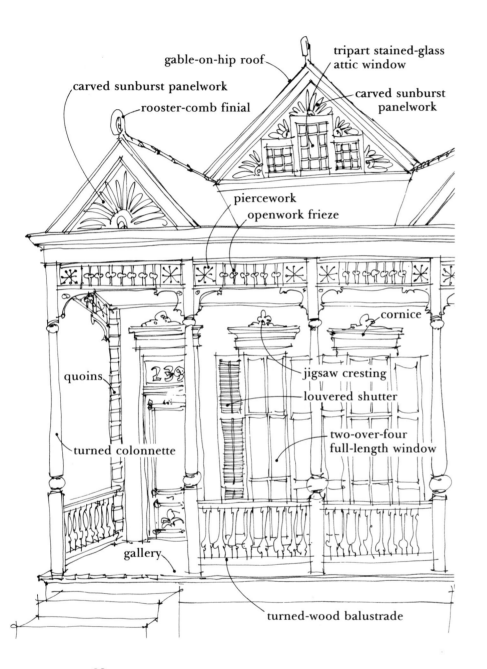

carved sunburst panelwork

gable-on-hip roof

tripart stained-glass attic window

rooster-comb finial

carved sunburst panelwork

piercework openwork frieze

cornice

quoins

jigsaw cresting

louvered shutter

turned colonnette

two-over-four full-length window

gallery

turned-wood balustrade

EASTLAKE SHOTGUN DOUBLE

Many neighborhoods in the city are lined with rows of wood-frame Eastlake shotguns on brick piers similar to this four-bay double. An openwork frieze (spindle band) with piercework, supported by decorative fan brackets, spans the space between turned colonnettes supporting a gable-on-hip roof. The roof is accentuated by smaller double gables flanking a center gable, with its tripart stained-glass attic window surrounded by carved sunburst panelwork; the smaller gables also feature sunburst-motif panelwork. Rooster-comb finials terminate all three gables. Entrances consist of decorative carved doors with stained-glass panels and transoms above.

Full-length gallery windows are two-over-four, with full louvered shutters. Both door and window casings have decorative moldings and are topped by ornate cornices and jigsaw cresting. Balusters are of the turned-wood type. Corner quoins terminate the drop siding on the front facade.

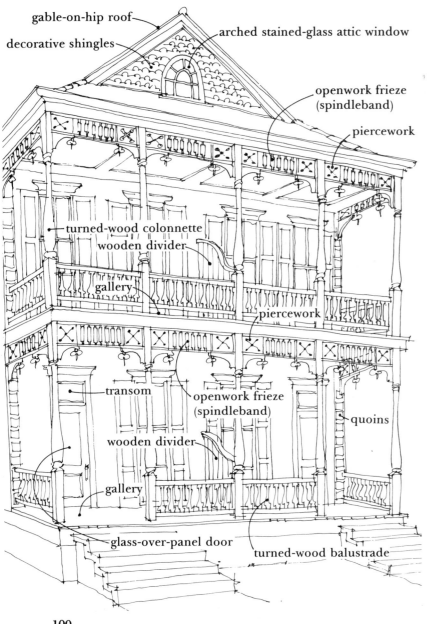

gable-on-hip roof

decorative shingles

arched stained-glass attic window

openwork frieze (spindleband)

piercework

turned-wood colonnette

wooden divider

gallery

piercework

transom

openwork frieze (spindleband)

quoins

wooden divider

gallery

glass-over-panel door

turned-wood balustrade

100

EASTLAKE DOUBLE-GALLERY SHOTGUN DOUBLE

A two-story shotgun double common in Late Victorian neighborhoods. The upper and lower galleries have identical decorative wood elements: turned wooden colonnettes, wooden balusters, and an openwork frieze composed of spindles, piercework, and fan brackets.

The front facade has a gable-on-hip roof penetrated by a stained-glass attic window surrounded by decorative shingles. Glass-over-panel entrance doors with transoms above flank two-over-four, double-hung windows at the first level. All windows on the upper front facade are also double-hung, two-over-four. A wooden divider separates the dwelling units at both the upper and lower galleries. (In some cases the front yards of shotgun doubles also have divided fenced areas.)

THE BRACKET STYLE (1880–1905)

The Bracket style is also referred to as the New Orleans Mill-work style and the Victorian Italianate style. The term *Bracket* is used here because it seems to characterize most clearly the main feature of the style: large brackets supporting a roof overhang above a gallery.

The origin of the style, found in greater numbers in New Orleans than anywhere else in the country, is uncertain. It appears to be a blending of Late Victorian ornamentation and Italianate brackets. Some two-story houses in the Italianate style also have large brackets supporting roof overhangs; however, the vertical length of these brackets is generally greater than the horizontal. With the proliferation of catalogue-ordered, prefabricated lathe and jigsaw work in the 1880s, the brackets took on different proportions (with the horizontal dimension becoming greater than the vertical) and embellishments common to the Victorian period, such as the popular sunburst.

The Bracket style incorporates ornamentation also common to the Eastlake and Queen Anne styles, popular during the same period, including turned balusters, decorative shingles in roof gables, and stained glass in doors and attic windows.

The style has a particularly close kinship with Eastlake; in fact, some two-story houses have first-level galleries with turned colonnettes and bracketed spindle bands in the Eastlake manner and Bracket-style second-level galleries. There are also examples of brackets incorporating a spindle band, as well as examples of spindle bands running between brackets.

By far the most common house types built in the Bracket style were shotgun singles and doubles with either hip or gable-on-hip roof overhangs. These overhangs, which varied from two to six feet, were most frequently four to five feet in depth. Bracket-style shotguns were generally of wood-frame construction with weatherboard siding, raised approximately three feet on brick piers. Drop siding was commonly used on the front facade in conjunction with corner quoins. Windows on the front facade were often full-length, double-hung, two-over-four, either flat-topped or segmentally arched in the Italianate manner. During their period of popularity it was not uncommon to add brackets to the roof overhangs of older houses such as Creole cottages in an attempt to update them.

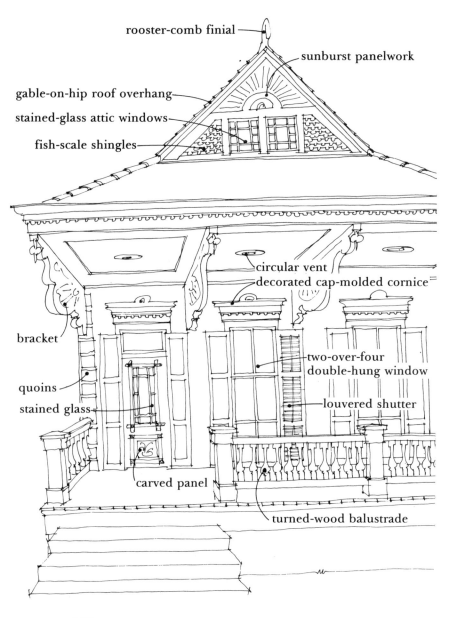

rooster-comb finial

sunburst panelwork

gable-on-hip roof overhang

stained-glass attic windows

fish-scale shingles

circular vent

decorated cap-molded cornice

bracket

quoins

stained glass

two-over-four double-hung window

louvered shutter

carved panel

turned-wood balustrade

BRACKET SHOTGUN SINGLE

One of the most common houses in New Orleans is this wood-frame Bracket shotgun. This three-bay single with a bracketed gable-on-hip roof overhang has a stained-glass door, a carved panel with a central sunburst motif, and paired stained-glass attic windows surrounded by decorative fish-scale shingles. The brackets, of the type found in the millwork catalogues of the late 1800s, are generally constructed of cypress.

The full-length, square-headed openings have simple surrounds, decorated cap-molded cornices, and operable louvered shutters. The front facade is further accentuated by drop siding (common weatherboard was used in most cases on the sides and rear) and corner quoins. The porch is enclosed by a decorative wood balustrade of turned balusters.

It is not uncommon to find three or four of these houses in a row, with identical facades, each painted a different color.

THE QUEEN ANNE STYLE (1880–1905)

British architect Richard Norman Shaw (1831–1912) is generally considered a major force in the creation of the Queen Anne style through his 1868 design of a house called Leyswood in Sussex, England. The style was introduced to Americans in the form of two buildings erected by the British government at the Philadelphia Exposition of 1876. The buildings were much admired by visitors and the style soon gained popularity throughout the U.S.

Queen Anne houses grew organically from the inside out, with the inner function and room arrangement giving form to the outer shell. The simple rectangular box of previous years was exploded and replaced by protrusions in the form of balconies, overhanging gables, towers, turrets, and wraparound porches. Asymmetry was the rule, with dormers, gables, and towers extending in all directions. Roofs were steep, with numerous gables, roof-peak ornaments, and different-sized dormers placed asymmetrically. Towers and turrets were round, octagonal, or square.

The main decorative feature of the style was texture, accomplished through variety and contrast in materials and ornamentation. Construction was generally wood frame on brick piers with weatherboard siding, with as many as three or four different types of decorative shingles frequently incorporated into a single design. Porches were supported by turned-wood or classical-influenced columns, the latter often paired and frequently mounted on pedestals. Porch and balcony balustrades were composed of decorative turned-wood balusters.

Ornamentation was abundant and varied. (In some instances Queen Anne absorbed Eastlake, with Queen Anne houses embellished with Eastlake ornamentation, primarily openwork frieze spindle bands, on porches and galleries.) Glass—beveled, stained, and etched in the Victorian manner—was an important design feature in Queen Anne houses, enhancing doors, transoms, and windows.

The most common paint colors were natural, autumnal, and earthy: maroon, red, orange, and green were popular. The body, trim, shutters, and window sashes of houses were often painted different colors, with as many as five contrasting but harmonious shades of warm reds, browns, deep greens, umbers, and golden ochres used on a single house. Large full-length windows on the front facade were often grouped together, without wood shutters.

Some Queen Anne houses are called "free classic" because of their use of Greek and Roman decorative motifs such as swags and garlands. The introduction of the Palladian window and classical columns in the Queen Anne style forecast the emerging trend toward the classical revival which was to become popular shortly after the turn of the century.

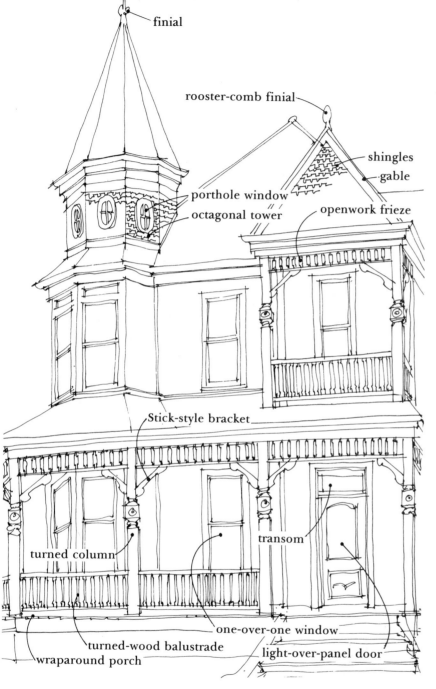

finial

rooster-comb finial

shingles

gable

porthole window

octagonal tower

openwork frieze

Stick-style bracket

transom

turned column

one-over-one window

turned-wood balustrade

light-over-panel door

wraparound porch

QUEEN ANNE HOUSE
WITH TOWER

This wood-frame Queen Anne house has an octagonal tower with porthole windows and a conical roof topped with a finial. The wraparound front porch is laced with an Eastlake-style openwork frieze of turned-wood spindles. The frieze is supported by Stick-style brackets; turned columns reach up to support the porch roof and an upper-level gallery with a steep front gable.

The porch balusters are turned wood. The entrance doorway has a glass upper light over a carved panel, with a transom above. Windows are large-pane, double-hung, one-over-one, a feature that developed in response to new technology that made large panes of glass available.

Fish-scale shingles adorn the front gable and upper part of the tower, while the remainder of the facade is covered with weatherboard siding.

L vogt-79

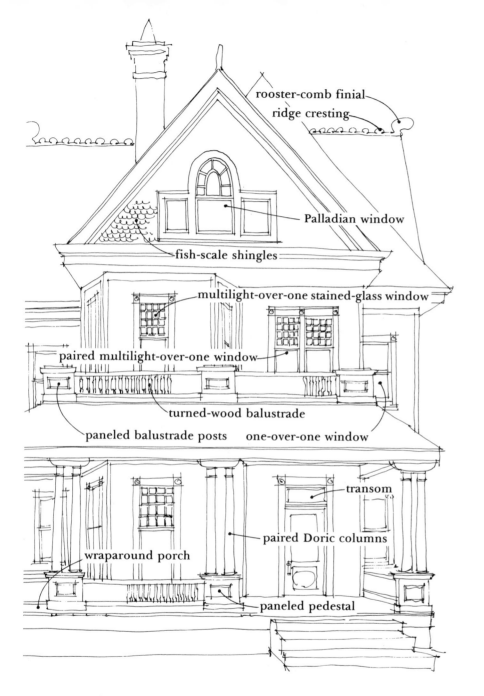

rooster-comb finial

ridge cresting

Palladian window

fish-scale shingles

multilight-over-one stained-glass window

paired multilight-over-one window

turned-wood balustrade

paneled balustrade posts   one-over-one window

transom

paired Doric columns

wraparound porch

paneled pedestal

QUEEN ANNE HOUSE

Although many Queen Anne houses in the city have towers, the majority do not. This multigabled Queen Anne has a generous wraparound porch supported by slender paired Doric columns mounted on paneled pedestals. Turned-wood balusters are utilized on the porch and on the second-level balcony, with balustrade posts to match the pedestals below. Multiple gables with ridge cresting and rooster-comb finials are pronounced visual elements. The front gable features a stained-glass Palladian-style window surrounded by fish-scale shingles. Weatherboard siding is used on the entire wood-frame structure.

The entrance consists of a transom above a door with a glass upper light and a carved lower panel. Some windows are one-over-one; others have a multilight, stained-glass upper sash over a single light below. Paired windows are visible in the front facade on the second level.

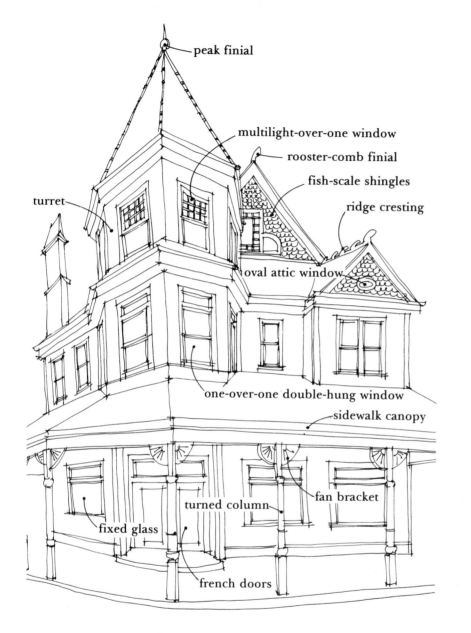

peak finial

multilight-over-one window

rooster-comb finial

fish-scale shingles

ridge cresting

turret

oval attic window

one-over-one double-hung window

sidewalk canopy

turned column

fan bracket

fixed glass

french doors

QUEEN ANNE CORNER STOREHOUSE

Storehouses, generally constructed in the popular styles of the era, are very common in New Orleans. This corner grocery store is typical of the commercial establishments constructed during the Victorian period.

The highly visible three-story corner turret is a major feature from which the rest of the building appears to radiate. A large roofed area supported by turned columns with fan brackets projects over the sidewalk to protect the entrance from the elements. The entrance has glass french doors, set at a forty-five degree angle and situated directly below the turret.

Large fixed-glass panes at the first level provide space for advertisements. The windows of the upper residential levels are double-hung, one-over-one or multilighted-over-one. Gables with rather steeply pitched roofs have rooster-comb finials and ridge cresting.

The building is wood frame with weatherboard siding and decorative fish-scale shingles on the gables.

L. Vogt 82

THE RICHARDSONIAN ROMANESQUE STYLE (1890–1910)

The Romanesque style, strongly influenced by Roman architecture and by Byzantine art, was prevalent in western Europe during the eleventh and twelfth centuries. American architects began experimenting with Romanesque design in the 1840s and 1850s, but it was Henry Hobson Richardson's creative interpretation that popularized the style throughout the United States.

Richardson, a great-grandson of Joseph Priestley (the discoverer of oxygen), was born in St. James Parish, Louisiana, in 1838. He spent much of his early childhood on the Priestley plantation and in New Orleans. After a year at the University of Louisiana he entered Harvard. He graduated in 1859 and traveled to Paris, where he attended the Ecole des Beaux-Arts. After five years in Paris he returned to America and started an architectural practice in New York City. In 1874 he moved to Boston, where his career prospered, and he received a continuing series of commissions. His acquaintances included the leading artists, scholars, and intellectuals of the time. By 1882 he was recognized as the leading architect in America. His health deteriorated toward the end of his life; he died in 1886, at the age of forty-seven, but his work continued to exert a tremendous influence on American architecture.

Richardson's buildings were more horizontal than Romanesque Revival designs by other American architects, and he used rough-textured stone as a major feature, supplanting the smooth stone typical of the style. This rock-faced masonry, usually composed of random-sized stones, gave the houses a feeling of great weight. Windows were recessed, with deep reveals further accentuating the heaviness, while contrasting smoother stones highlighted lintels or arches. Rectangular windows were often divided into rectangular lights, and it is not unusual to find square-headed and arch-headed windows in the same facade. Also common are Syrian arches—supported by clustered columns with cubiform capitals enriched with foliated forms—frequently creating an arcade.

The overall appearance is one of balance, but likely to be asymmetrical. Very steeply gabled wall dormers are prominent; roof dormers, when used, are usually of a low profile and sometimes of the eyebrow type (although this type was not very common in New Orleans).

Romanesque houses were constructed in the city around the turn of the century, but the style was not widespread because it was used primarily for large mansions. In other parts of the country it was more frequently used in the design of public, commercial, and religious buildings.

one-over-one window

wall dormer

hip roof

rooftop deck

finial

transomed one-over-one window

tripart arched windows

Syrian-arch arcade

rock-faced masonry

smooth-stone highlight

porch

RICHARDSONIAN ROMANESQUE HOUSE

This large Richardsonian Romanesque house, with rock-faced masonry on all exterior walls, typifies the heaviness characteristic of the style.

The 2½-story house, slightly raised, is capped with a steeply pitched hip roof. Wall dormers piercing the roof on all sides are topped with gable finials at the peak and sides.

A large porch enclosed by an arcade projects from the facade and supports a rooftop deck. All arched openings are highlighted by smooth stone contrasting with the rock-faced stone of the walls. Window openings are one-over-one with transoms on the second level and one-over-one in the wall dormers. Tripart arched windows are used in the front and side at the second level.

THE EARLY TWENTIETH CENTURY (1900–1940)

The twentieth century promised the American family a new way of life. The industrial economy was expanding, providing job opportunities throughout the country and initiating a consumer revolution. Automobiles, chain stores, telephones, movie palaces, and installment buying would soon become commonplace. In New Orleans the port was prospering, jazz was evolving, and the city was enjoying grand opera, theater, and vaudeville.

With the pressures of an increasing population ever present, the search continued for new options for development. The screw pump, invented around the turn of the century by A. Baldwin Wood, a gifted New Orleans engineer, was a major technological breakthrough that would allow tremendous expansion throughout the city. This heavy-duty pump could raise huge volumes of water very quickly. It made possible the development of a modern, comprehensive drainage system, thus opening large areas of land—primarily swamps—which up until this time had formed the northern boundary of the city and had been considered uninhabitable.

Wood's expertise did not go unnoticed. Widely recognized for his achievements, he assisted both Holland and the Dutch East Indies in solving their drainage problems.

The original legislation permitting construction of the new pumping system was passed in 1899. In addition to the pumps, miles of canals had to be dug to carry the water to pumping stations, where it would be lifted to other canals flowing into Lake Borgne or Lake Pontchartrain. Extensive levee construction was required to complete the system. Draining these low-lying areas proved to be a tremendous task, requiring large investments of both time and money, and for many years growth was gradual and scattered.

Even after the drainage system was completed, the newly created land was not without problems. Soil subsidence resulting from the drainage process caused numerous construction difficulties; the city's residents were learning—often the hard way—that swamp soils had the highly undesirable characteristic of sinking after being drained. Areas with an elevation of about sea level often dropped considerably below that once the water was removed. But despite the expense involved, development continued to creep northward toward Lake Pontchartrain, the pace quickening with the economic boom of the 1920s.

New Orleanians had been plagued by yellow fever throughout the 1800s, completely ignorant of its cause. In 1905 yellow fever again broke out in the city. But this time things were different. The Aedes aegypti mosquito had recently been proven to be the carrier, and the city mounted an all-out attack against the culprit. Some 68,000 cisterns were screened and over 700 miles of open gutters and drains were oiled or salted. Within a very short time the outbreak was curtailed, putting an end to a dreaded chapter in the city's history.

For many years street railways were the primary means of transportation in New Orleans. In 1893 the first electric cars were introduced. By 1910 four companies were operating a network of twenty-eight lines with more than 170 miles of tracks spread out over the entire developed area of the city.

After World War I the cotton trade in New Orleans declined as India and Egypt began to compete in the marketplace and the boll weevil and exhausted soils took their toll at home. But Latin American imports increased: Americans were heavy coffee drinkers, and after the turn of the century banana imports also rose sharply. New Orleans was the chief port of entry for both of these cargoes.

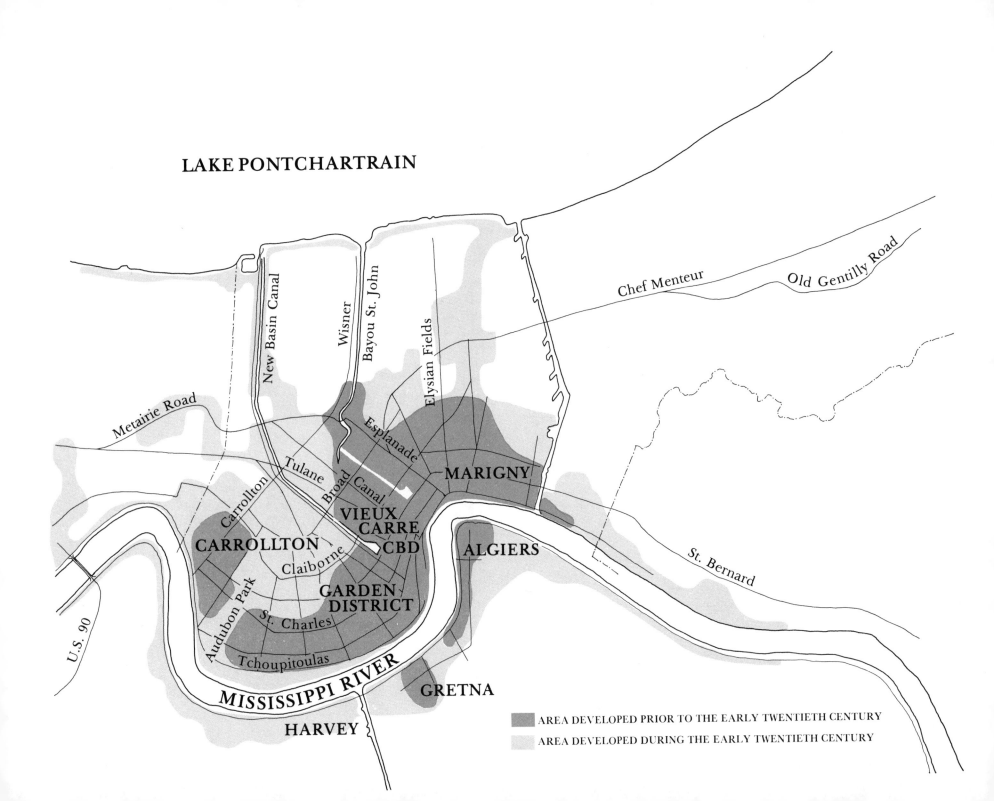

LAKE PONTCHARTRAIN

Chef Menteur

Old Gentilly Road

New Basin Canal

Wisner

Bayou St. John

Elysian Fields

Metairie Road

Esplanade

MARIGNY

Tulane

Broad

Canal

Carrollton

VIEUX
CARRE

CBD

CARROLLTON

ALGIERS

St. Bernard

Claiborne

Audubon Park

GARDEN
DISTRICT

St. Charles

Tchoupitoulas

U.S. 90

MISSISSIPPI RIVER

GRETNA

HARVEY

AREA DEVELOPED PRIOR TO THE EARLY TWENTIETH CENTURY

AREA DEVELOPED DURING THE EARLY TWENTIETH CENTURY

Along with the new technology of drainage pumps, automobiles, and steel bridges, the twentieth century brought with it new ideals in architecture. The tastemakers again looked to the past for inspiration. The elaborate texture and visual gymnastics of the Victorian period were replaced by a general feeling of restraint, expressed in Georgian Colonial Revival and Neoclassical Revival and in numerous other eclectic styles including Beaux Arts Classicism, Neoitalianate, Italian Renaissance, and Dutch Colonial Revival.

Georgian Colonial and Neoclassical Revival houses were most often painted all white, a sharp contrast to the vibrant colors of the Victorian era. Turned-wood columns were supplanted by the classical orders, and stained glass lost its popularity.

Construction boomed in the 1920s. The new prosperity heralded the appearance of two new styles by way of California: the Bungalow and Spanish Colonial Revival. The Tudor Revival style, with its half-timbering and stucco infill, also enjoyed limited popularity in the city during this period.

As development spread and approached Lake Pontchartrain, it became increasingly obvious that the lakefront levee was inadequate to protect the growing city from flooding in the event of a major hurricane. To deal with this situation, the Orleans Levee District was created in 1924. The state legislature empowered the board of commissioners of the levee district to develop and execute a plan that would upgrade the levee while making the lakefront more attractive. A concrete seawall was constructed, 5½ miles long and approximately 3,000 feet out from the existing shoreline, and the area in between was filled with material pumped from the lake bottom to a level varying from five to ten feet, making the approximately 2,000 acres of newly created land some of the highest in the city. For over two hundred years New Orleans residents had been building a barrier between the city and the river by constructing warehouses directly on the riverfront. With the creation of this new land the city suddenly had a new municipal airport and a clean public waterfront lined with beaches, boulevards, and parks. These amenities were enthusiastically received and served as a great catalyst for development.

Throughout the 1920s the city spread to the north, south, and east as the population continued to grow. This expansion was facilitated by new bus routes and by the increased mobility provided by the automobile. The Huey P. Long Bridge upriver from the city was completed in 1933, allowing automobiles and trains easy access to the West Bank, which up until this time had been accessible only by ferry.

But the Great Depression soon brought growth to a standstill, and the levee board found itself in serious financial trouble. The Federal Works Progress Administration (WPA) stepped in, taking over most of the projects the levee board had been unable to complete. During the late 1930s most construction in the city, including work on streets, sewers, drainage, water, recreation facilities, canal maintenance, levees, and public buildings, was done under the auspices of the WPA. At the same time trouble was brewing in Europe; America observed anxiously as the seeds of World War II were sown.

THE GEORGIAN COLONIAL REVIVAL (1890–1920)

During the late nineteenth century a revived interest in American colonial architecture swept the country. One of the reasons for the shift to colonial revivalism was a reaction to the excesses and complexities of the Victorian aesthetic that had dominated American taste for almost forty years. At the same time a patriotic mood was growing, inspired by the renewed interest in America's past generated by the Centennial celebrations of 1876. Along with this patriotic mood came the desire for a distinctively American architecture.

The Georgian Colonial Revival movement started in the Northeast in the late 1880s with two houses designed by the architectural firm of McKim, Mead, and White. The style received a great deal of exposure at the Columbian Exposition of 1893 in Chicago, where it was featured in a number of buildings. Millions of visitors returned home from the fair wanting to emulate what they had seen.

Some Georgian Colonial Revival houses were attempts at constructing replicas of Georgian houses built on the Eastern Seaboard during the English colonial period (1700–1770), while others more closely resembled the asymmetrical houses of the Victorian period embellished with colonial detailing. Georgian Colonial houses had been inspired by the work of Italian architect Andrea Palladio, whose *Four Books of Architecture,* published in Venice in 1570, had had a profound effect throughout Europe. In England, where the style originated, Georgian houses reflected Renaissance ideals popularized by Sir Christopher Wren and Inigo Jones.

The most common plan for Georgian Colonial Revival houses was the two-story, five-bay, center-hall Georgian design, with a stairway to the second level located in the center hall. The basic form was square or rectangular; characteristics included symmetrically placed windows, Palladian windows, hipped or side-gable roofs of medium pitch, and porticoes with classical columns. Fanlight transoms and triangular pediments were also common, as were sidelights flanking the entrance door. Porches were occasionally asymmetrically placed. Classical ornamentation included garlands, swags, dentils, and bracketed cornices. Dormers and porticoes were frequently capped with swan-neck pediments, and a common decorative feature was the Grecian urn–shaped finial placed on top of balustrade posts. Balustrades were generally turned wood, but much more attenuated than in the previous era.

Georgian Colonial Revival houses were most often constructed of exposed brick, stucco, or wood frame with weatherboard siding. Classical pilasters were sometimes used at the corners.

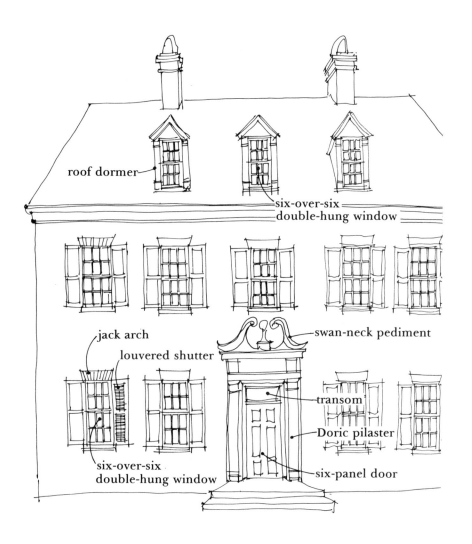

roof dormer

six-over-six
double-hung window

jack arch

louvered shutter

swan-neck pediment

transom

Doric pilaster

six-over-six
double-hung window

six-panel door

GEORGIAN COLONIAL REVIVAL HOUSE

Typical of Georgian Colonial Revival houses is this two-story, five-bay, center-hall house. Constructed of brick, it has symmetrically placed six-over-six, double-hung windows with louvered shutters. A medium-pitched side-gable roof is pierced by two interior chimneys and three pedimented dormers with six-over-six windows and Doric pilasters.

The transomed six-panel wooden door is slightly recessed in an entranceway composed of Doric pilasters supporting a plain entablature topped with a swan-neck pediment. Set back from the street, the house is reached by a wide brick walk.

The likeliest color combination for this house is red brick, white windows and trim, and green shutters.

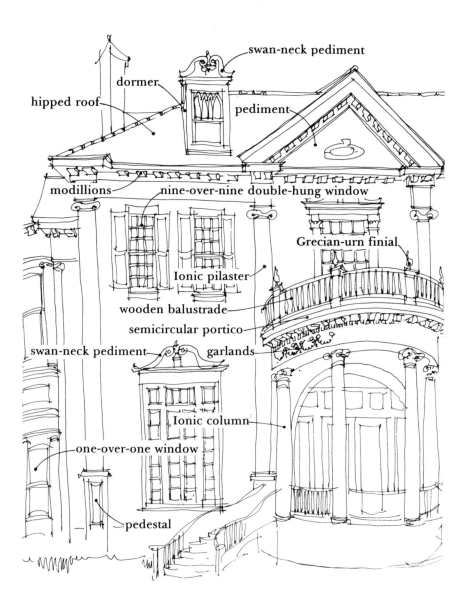

swan-neck pediment

dormer

hipped roof

pediment

modillions

nine-over-nine double-hung window

Grecian-urn finial

Ionic pilaster

wooden balustrade

semicircular portico

swan-neck pediment

garlands

Ionic column

one-over-one window

pedestal

126

GEORGIAN COLONIAL REVIVAL HOUSE

A semicircular portico centered in the front facade of this two-story frame house has Ionic columns supporting a circular balcony above. The house has a Georgian five-bay center-hall plan, with the first floor substituting multilight french doors with sidelights for the two double-hung windows on the second floor. As a result the first level has a three-bay facade.

The delicate wood balustrade features posts topped by wooden finials in the form of Grecian urns. Monumental Ionic pilasters on pedestals are applied to the front facade and support a classical pediment rising from a hipped roof.

Multilight windows, doors, and transoms are utilized as well as one-over-one windows. Swan-neck pediments appear in the front facade over the full-length casement windows at the first level, the central window at the second level, and the symmetrically placed dormers projecting from the roof.

There are modillions in the cornice of the porch, roof, and central pediment. The house is clad in weatherboard siding.

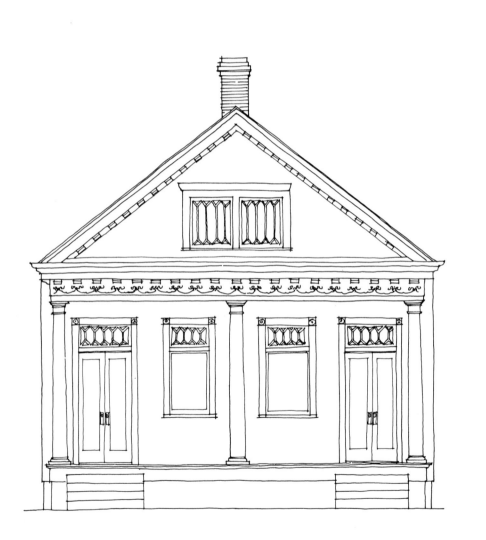

THE NEOCLASSICAL REVIVAL (1895–1920)

The World's Columbian Exposition in Chicago in 1893 affected the taste of the American public for a generation. It featured architect Daniel Burnham's famous White City and Neoclassical Revival buildings by Charles B. Atwood and by the firm of McKim, Mead, and White, who designed in both the Greek and Roman orders. The exposition was an overwhelming success, attracting more than 27 million visitors.

One of the most striking aspects of the fair's architecture was the all-white color scheme. After years of dark, heavy colors, the Late Victorian eye was immediately attracted to the all-white look of the new classicism: the "American Renaissance" was born.

Neoclassical Revival houses began to appear on the streets of New Orleans in the late 1890s and were constructed for approximately thirty years. The style served as an inspiration for houses of all sizes and in all price ranges. The larger houses were very classical in appearance, with massive porticoes as their central feature; in some cases the house was a temple form. The smaller houses—primarily single and double shotguns—were constructed with gabled front galleries supported by three columns, generally of the unfluted Doric order.

Neoclassical Revival houses represented a return to the rectangular, with none of the projections and varied roof lines common in the Victorian era. Porches and galleries were used on the front facade only.

A semicircular window in the pediment was a very common feature, as was a semicircular fanlight over the front door. Other characteristics of the style include modified-diamond-paned windows and a single, centrally placed hipped-roof dormer projecting from a hipped roof supported by three classical columns. Porch balustrades were either metal or wood. Most Neoclassical Revival houses were either stucco or wood frame on brick piers with weatherboard siding; they were generally painted all white.

Although heavy ornamentation had faded almost completely from the design vocabulary by this time, a number of very ornate examples of Neoclassical Revival houses can be found in New Orleans.

Many houses constructed in the city during this period have classical ornamentation but neither a Georgian center-hall plan nor a Neoclassical temple form. In such cases it is very difficult to determine which of the two styles the house reflects.

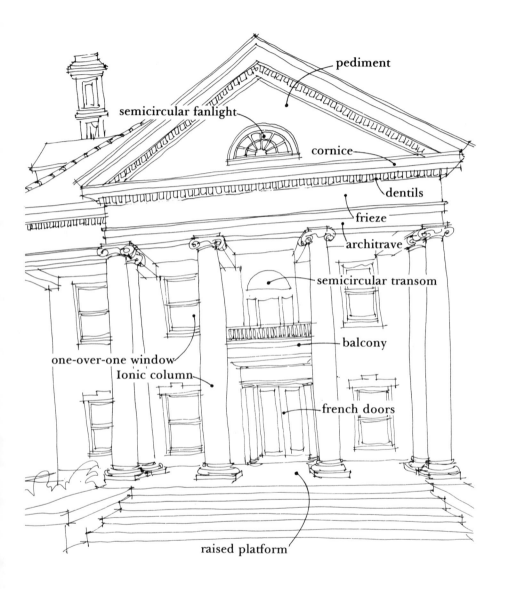

pediment

semicircular fanlight

cornice

dentils

frieze

architrave

semicircular transom

balcony

one-over-one window

Ionic column

french doors

raised platform

NEOCLASSICAL REVIVAL CENTER-HALL HOUSE

Massive Ionic columns support a simple, restrained, denticulated entablature and pediment with a semicircular fanlight, creating a generous portico projecting from a gallery on this large Neoclassical Revival residence. Although the house has a five-bay center-hall plan in the Georgian manner, the imposing Greek-temple form establishes it as Neoclassical Revival.

The entrance features french doors flanked by Doric pilasters situated below a small balcony with glass doors topped with a semicircular transom. The windows are large, double-hung, one-over-one, a feature that clearly dates this house as Neoclassical Revival rather than Greek Revival; during the Greek Revival era six-over-six windows were generally used.

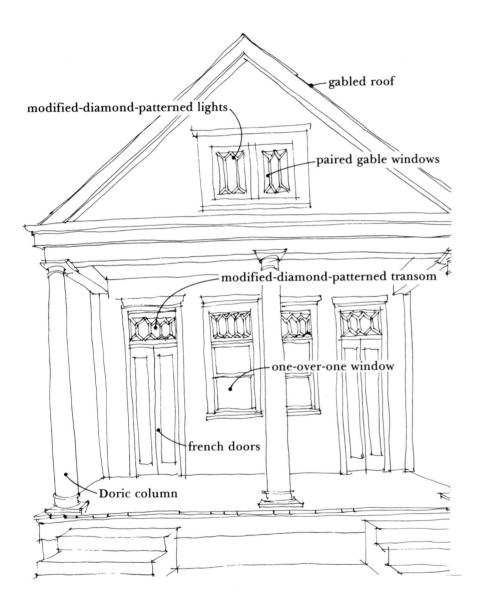

gabled roof

modified-diamond-patterned lights

paired gable windows

modified-diamond-patterned transom

one-over-one window

french doors

Doric column

NEOCLASSICAL REVIVAL SHOTGUN DOUBLE

This small, unassuming, four-bay Neoclassical Revival shotgun double clearly expresses the end of the Victorian era; its simplicity much more closely resembles the Greek Revival designs of the 1840s than the heavily ornamented style favored by the Victorians.

The three unfluted columns, a trademark of small Neoclassical Revival houses, are of the Doric order. They support a high gabled roof resembling a pediment, with paired gable windows divided by modified-diamond-patterned lights. The entrance features narrow french doors with a modified-diamond-paned glass transom, repeated above the adjacent one-over-one windows. The house is wood frame with weatherboard siding on brick piers.

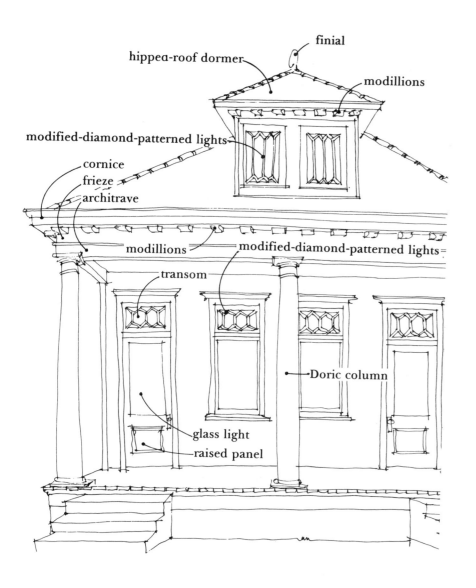

finial

hippea-roof dormer

modillions

modified-diamond-patterned lights

cornice
frieze
architrave

modillions

modified-diamond-patterned lights

transom

Doric column

glass light

raised panel

NEOCLASSICAL REVIVAL SHOTGUN DOUBLE

A one-story, wood-frame shotgun double on piers, with a hipped roof supported by three simple Doric columns and a single hipped-roof dormer with paired windows. These windows, like the front-facade windows and the transoms over the entrance doors, have modified-diamond panes. The front doors have a large single light above a raised panel.

Classical modillions appear under the cornice and the dormer roof eave. The facade is highlighted by very narrow weatherboard siding, while the sides and rear are most likely to be standard-size weatherboard.

134

THE TUDOR REVIVAL (1910–1930)

The Tudor Revival borrowed its inspiration from the houses that evolved in the Tudor era in England (1485–1558). The Black Death of the fourteenth century had left England with a population reduced by a third and huge tracts of farmland lying unattended. Because of the demand for wool in the Netherlands, much of this farmland was turned over to the raising of sheep, and a great national export trade in wool developed.

The wool merchants made huge fortunes and power slowly passed from the lords to these merchants and tradesmen. As their new prosperity generated a need for better housing for a greater number of people, emphasis slowly shifted from security to comfort: houses became larger, more fireplaces were added, and windows grew more numerous and bigger as England revived its glass-making industry, dormant through most of the Dark Ages.

One characteristic common to Tudor houses—and copied in Tudor Revival buildings—was the jettied upper floor (a projecting floor that jutted out above the lower level). The jetty served a number of functions. During this time houses were constructed with the wide dimension of the floorboards of the upper floors laid flat, often resulting in floors that sagged. By projecting the floorboards slightly beyond the wall support, the builder could place the upper wall to act as a counterbalance, providing a more rigid structure. This technique also served to protect the lower floor from rain and snow, and in crowded city conditions it allowed for larger houses on small lots.

The distinguishing characteristics of the Tudor Revival style are high-pitched gabled roofs and half-timber construction with stucco infill. The half-timbering is usually accentuated by the contrast between white stucco and the very dark or black exposed timbers. Frequently the half-timbering is used as a decorative element, creating patterns in the facade.

Windows with small diamond-shaped panes were often used in the upper sash of double-hung windows, with a large single pane in the lower sash. Bay windows were also very common. Some of the more elaborate examples of the style have an attached porch with an arcade constructed of Tudor Gothic arches, usually in dark red brick.

Tudor Revival was not extremely popular in New Orleans, but there are a number of examples scattered throughout the city.

Lavenham, England, c. 1529

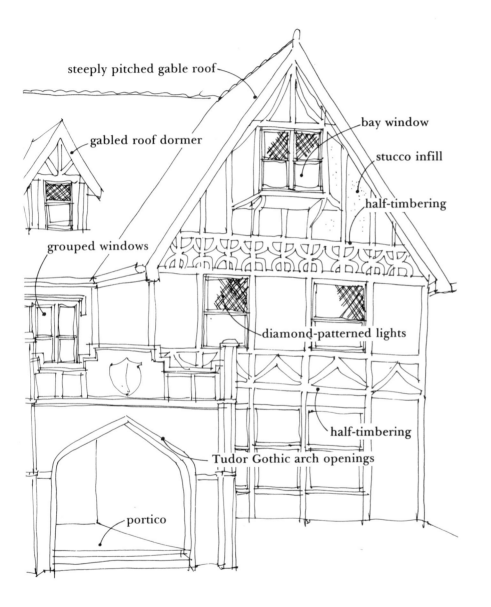

steeply pitched gable roof

gabled roof dormer

bay window

stucco infill

half-timbering

grouped windows

diamond-patterned lights

half-timbering

Tudor Gothic arch openings

portico

TUDOR REVIVAL HOUSE

This Tudor Revival house has the style's characteristic steeply pitched gables and Tudor Gothic arches in the portico. Half-timbering is a distinguishing visual feature. Its effect is accentuated by the contrast between the dark timber members and the white stucco infill; geometric patterns are created by this contrast.

Windows are either single or grouped. The upper sashes of many of the windows are divided into small multilights in a diamond pattern, while the lower sashes consist of single panes of glass. A bay window projects from the prominent front gable, and a small single dormer with half-timbering is centered in the first of a pair of side gables.

The front portico, placed to one side of the facade, is constructed of brick.

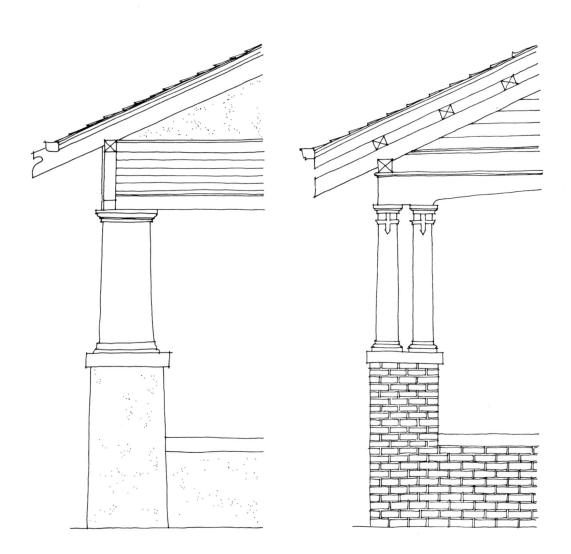
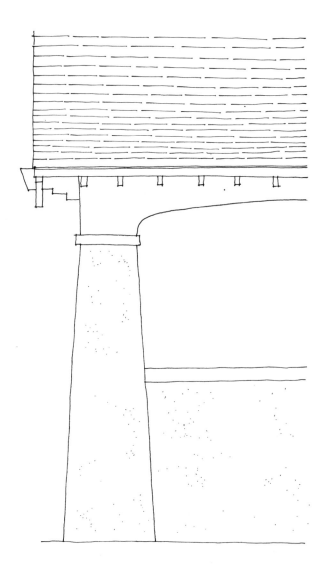

THE BUNGALOW STYLE (1910–1940)

During the early 1900s a new house style developed in California. Within a very short time, aided by widely circulated plan books, it had spread throughout the country. The style, known as "Bungalow" (it is also sometimes referred to as the "California style"), was very popular in New Orleans throughout the twenties and thirties.

The name "bungalow" was derived from the Hindustani *bangla,* low houses surrounded by porches supposedly built in India by the English government as rest houses for foreign travelers. The term was brought back to England by retiring civil servants. The style fit comfortably with the Arts and Crafts movement that had originated in the late 1800s in Europe in response to the ugliness and urban squalor resulting from growing industrialism. The movement espoused the avoidance of machine-produced ornamentation, favoring simpler, hand-crafted elements—elements that could generally be fashioned with a carpenter's saw on the construction site.

Also influential were a number of other styles, including Stick, Japanese, and Swiss Chalet. The Bungalow's suitability for the mild climate combined with the Californian's willingness to experiment with new ideas to make it the ideal of the casual California life-style. Two of the leading architects of the style were Charles and Henry Greene, brothers whose practice centered in Pasadena, California.

In most cases Bungalows were one-story or 1½-story structures with low, simple lines and large projecting roofs with exposed roof rafters in the eaves. Construction was wood frame on brick piers with weatherboard siding, wood shingles, or stucco. It is quite common to find weatherboard siding on the main body of a house with stucco, or a combination of wood siding and stucco, on the porch. In the side-gable version, a large single roof dormer with either a shed or gable roof was commonly placed in the front facade. Porches and galleries were essential design features. Many Bungalows were originally built with screened porches, utilizing the newly developed insect screen. As more effective mosquito control reduced the threat posed by this annual summer menace, the screens gradually deteriorated and were not replaced.

Porch roofs were most often supported by large, tapered, square pedestals—usually of brick, stucco, or natural rock—extending approximately three feet above the porch level, with straight or tapered wooden posts on top. Frequently these wooden posts were paired, and tripled at the corners. Windows were double-hung or casement, often paired, with small panes divided into various patterns, some highly ordered and some random but generally arranged differently from those of any previous style. The Bungalow eliminated the window shutter from New Orleans residential construction, replacing it with the insect screen.

The style expressed a feeling of simplicity, a choice of comfort over elegance. There are thousands of Bungalows throughout New Orleans, in many cases dominating entire neighborhoods.

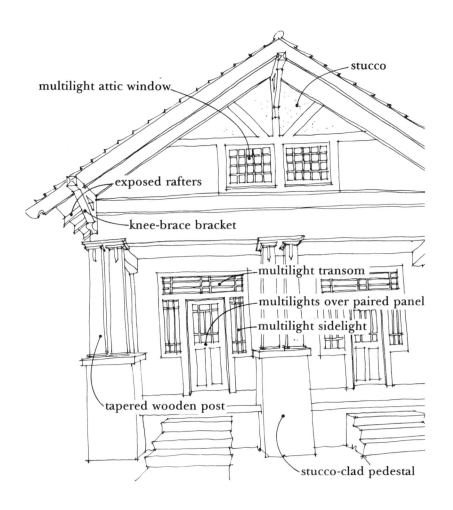

multilight attic window

stucco

exposed rafters

knee-brace bracket

multilight transom

multilights over paired panel

multilight sidelight

tapered wooden post

stucco-clad pedestal

BUNGALOW SHOTGUN DOUBLE

A very common sight in many parts of the city, this wood-frame Bungalow on brick piers has a front gallery shaded by a gabled roof.

A pair of multilight attic windows pierce the front gable and are surrounded by narrow weatherboard siding on both sides, a wide wooden beam band at the bottom, and exposed wooden members with stucco infill above. The roof structure is supported by paired, slightly tapered wooden posts, tripled at the corners, resting on stucco-clad pedestals.

The roof eaves have exposed rafters; the overhang on the front facade is supported by knee-brace wooden brackets. The entrances consist of multilight glass doors over panels, with multilight sidelights and transoms.

The exterior walls are clad in weatherboard siding. To the left of the house is a double-strip concrete driveway to accommodate the automobile, which was fast becoming a feature of family life during this period.

L. Vogt 82

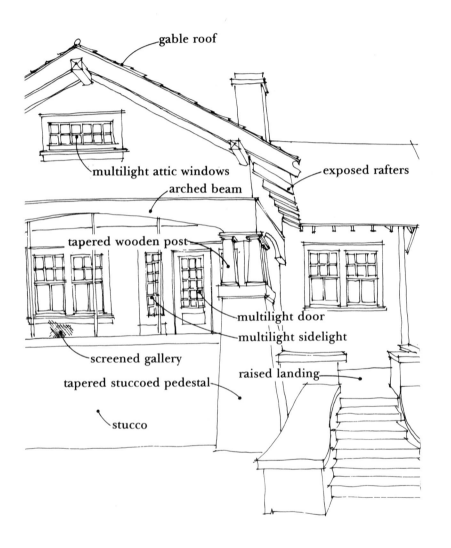

gable roof

multilight attic windows

arched beam

exposed rafters

tapered wooden post

multilight door

multilight sidelight

screened gallery

tapered stuccoed pedestal

raised landing

stucco

RAISED BUNGALOW

A raised one-story, wood-frame Bungalow with a screened gallery. Screen porches and galleries were common during the Bungalow era, although most have been removed from existing houses.

Wide, flared stuccoed steps approach the raised landing leading into the gallery. The roof consists of two simple, intersecting, low-pitched gables with exposed rafters. The front gable has a single multilight attic window surrounded by narrow weatherboard siding. A pair of massive, tapered, stuccoed pedestals support short, tapered, wooden posts, which in turn support the slightly arched beam spanning the screen-enclosed opening.

The entrance doorway has multilight sidelights around a multilight glass door. The entranceway is flanked by paired six-over-two, wood-framed, double-hung windows. The exterior walls are clad in weatherboard siding.

144

BUNGALOW

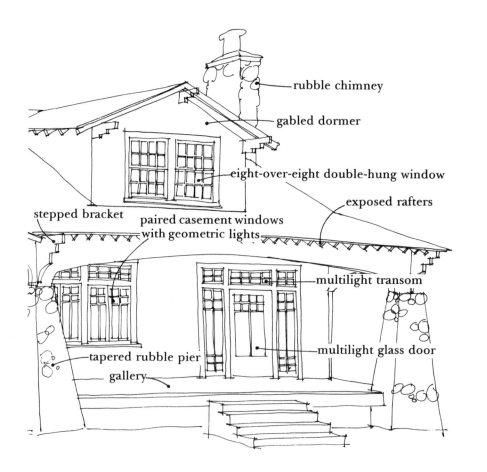

rubble chimney

gabled dormer

eight-over-eight double-hung window

exposed rafters

stepped bracket

paired casement windows
with geometric lights

multilight transom

tapered rubble pier

gallery

multilight glass door

A 1½-story wood-frame Bungalow with a broad gallery supported at each end by tapered rubble piers. A large dormer with paired multilight, double-hung windows centered in the roof is a major feature of the front facade (most Bungalow attics were unfinished and used only for storage).

The entranceway consists of a glass door with geometric divisions and matching sidelights and transoms. This geometric motif is also utilized in single and paired windows and in transoms on all fenestrations.

Stepped brackets support the side gable overhang and roof rafters are exposed in the eaves of the gallery roof. A sidewall chimney of rubble matching the front piers rises above the roof. The house, slightly raised on brick piers, is sided with weatherboard.

The plan of this Bungalow would most likely be a refinement of the Creole cottage plan, adapted to keep pace with the introduction of interior plumbing and the incorporation of the kitchen into the house. (This basic plan is also common among contemporary two-bedroom apartments in multifamily apartment buildings.)

THE SPANISH COLONIAL REVIVAL (1920–1940)

The Spanish Colonial Revival style was first introduced to millions of Americans at the 1915 Panama-California Exposition in San Diego, for which Bertram Grosvenor Goodhue served as chief architect. The style used as its models the missions and houses built by Spanish colonists in Florida and the Southwest rather than that of Spanish Colonial New Orleans.

Because of its radical departure from other common styles in the city, Spanish Colonial Revival is relatively easy to identify. Red barrel-tile roofs and stucco walls, usually painted white, impart a recognizable Spanish feeling. Any number of different stucco textures might be used, although rarely was more than one texture used on a particular house. Roofs were low-pitched, sometimes flat, with parapets capped with barrel tile.

Carved or cast ornaments, concentrated primarily around windows and doors, adorn most Spanish Colonial Revival houses. A highly ornate treatment of the main entrance was common, with an elaborate parapet extending above the roof line to draw attention to the entrance; the entrance itself was frequently recessed under a small porch.

Pilasters and arches supported by Moorish columns were other common design features. Balconies with wrought-iron railings were also common, although in some cases what appear to be iron-railed balconies were only decorative window treatments. Windows varied in size, and were often placed asymmetrically. When window grilles were used they were made of either turned wooden spindles or wrought iron. Arched windows of the casement type and fanlight transoms were frequent features.

Floor plans varied considerably, with no particular house type common to the style. The most common exterior wall material was stucco, with weatherboard siding and brick used less frequently.

Spanish Colonial Revival characteristics were also frequently combined with Bungalow features, creating houses best described as Spanish Colonial Bungalows.

SPANISH COLONIAL REVIVAL HOUSE

This house with low-pitched barrel-tile roof features a decorative parapet with pierced grillwork and ball finials above a recessed entranceway topped by a decorative cornice. The front door has a multilight glass panel and a transom above. The windows are of the multilight casement type. Glass french doors in the front facade have fanlight transoms above.

The gabled front wall has a circular vent with grillwork over a tripart window grouping terminated by a sculptured lintel. The barrel-tile roof creates a highly textured contrast to the smooth stucco walls of the facade.

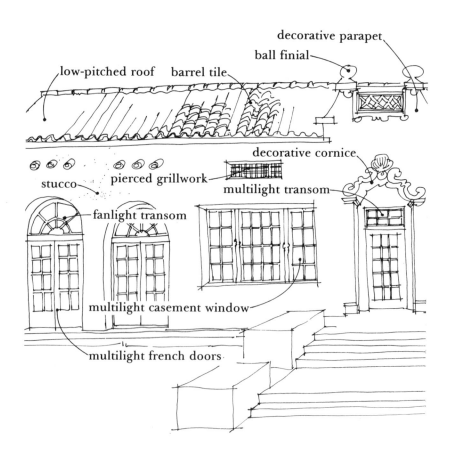

decorative parapet

ball finial

low-pitched roof   barrel tile

decorative cornice

stucco   pierced grillwork

multilight transom

fanlight transom

multilight casement window

multilight french doors

150

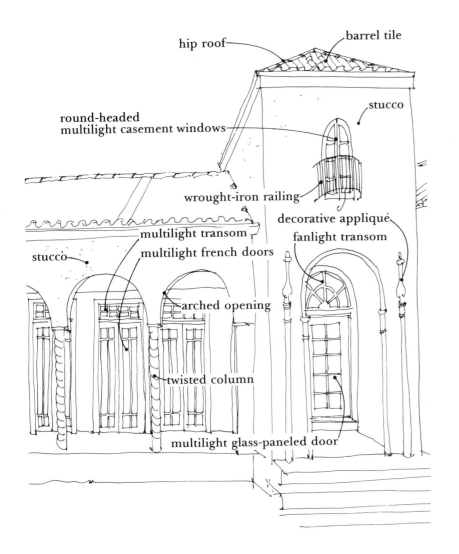

hip roof

barrel tile

stucco

round-headed
multilight casement windows

wrought-iron railing

decorative appliqué

multilight transom

fanlight transom

stucco

multilight french doors

arched opening

twisted column

multilight glass-paneled door

SPANISH COLONIAL REVIVAL HOUSE

A symbolic bell tower with a hip roof is the central feature of this Spanish Colonial Revival house. The entranceway—a multilight glass-paneled door and fanlight transom—is recessed into the tower.

The exterior walls are smooth stucco. The roof is covered with clay barrel tiles. French doors with matching transoms lie behind an arcade of arches supported by twisted columns. Wrought-iron railings used as decoration encircle round-headed, multilight casement windows in both the tower and the upper level of the gabled facade.

THE MODERN PERIOD (1940–)

With the onset of World War II prosperity returned to New Orleans, but construction was limited as the country turned its attention to the manufacture of war-related products, thus creating a severe shortage of building materials. When the war ended building activity in the city began to revive.

New Orleans had been struggling since the Civil War to rebuild its river trade; by 1945 she had regained her position as the second largest port in the United States. But competition among port cities remained fierce, and a new concept—container transportation—was rapidly revolutionizing the shipping industry. The idea was a simple one: shipping in standard-size metal boxes that could be transferred from a ship to a truck or a train flatcar easily and quickly. The port of New Orleans kept pace with the changing times and simultaneously maintained a substantial amount of traditional shipping trade because of its ongoing commerce with the underdeveloped countries of Latin America, where modern container vessels were not yet available. Shipping remained the city's principal industry, although tourism and the oil industry were also beginning to boost the economy.

During the 1940s comprehensive planning in New Orleans intensified, with new efforts directed at correcting some of the problems caused by urban growth and an increasing number of automobiles. A plan for the unification and consolidation of the city's railroads was approved in an effort to afford relief to the automobile-train grade-crossing conflict. Seven railroads were joined into one system, and 144 grade crossings were eliminated by construction of 22 major street grade separations, providing safer road conditions and allowing increased automotive mobility. At this time the International style, which had evolved in Europe during the 1920s, was beginning to make its presence felt in the city, primarily in the design of nonresidential buildings.

The 1950s joined renewed construction impetus with new American ideals: the automobile and a home in the suburbs were rapidly becoming the nation's status symbols. In 1950 the New Basin Canal (constructed in the 1830s) was filled, providing a right-of-way corridor for part of the interstate highway system then in the planning stage. The automobile had become an increasingly important factor in the everyday lives of New Orleanians, and improvement programs aimed at streets, highways, and bridges had increased its efficiency manyfold. The Greater New Orleans Bridge was completed in 1955, providing an automobile link from the Central Business District to Algiers and other areas of the West Bank.

The road was now paved, so to speak, for a mass exodus to the suburbs. Although the origins of suburban planning cannot be traced to a single source, it was strongly influenced by the philosophies of Frank Lloyd Wright's Broadacre City in the 1930s. Wright's plan proposed houses on one-acre lots in wooded settings on the fringes of urban areas. The plan clearly required that each family own an automobile.

During the 1930s and 1940s, development in New Orleans had occurred for the most part through the filling in of previously undeveloped land within the city. In the 1950s this situation began to change, with new growth suddenly spreading in all directions. Improved transportation routes, cheap gas, and the lure of less expensive land and lower taxes attracted large numbers of people to Jefferson Parish and the West Bank. This migration generated new taxes for Jefferson Parish, and local officials responded by building levees and streets as fast as the revenues accumulated. As a part of this process the new multilaned Veterans Memorial Highway was constructed, cutting straight across Jefferson to St. Charles Parish and further facilitating growth. Moisant Airfield was built and soon renamed New Orleans International Airport. Another major undertaking—the Pontchartrain Causeway—stretched twenty-four

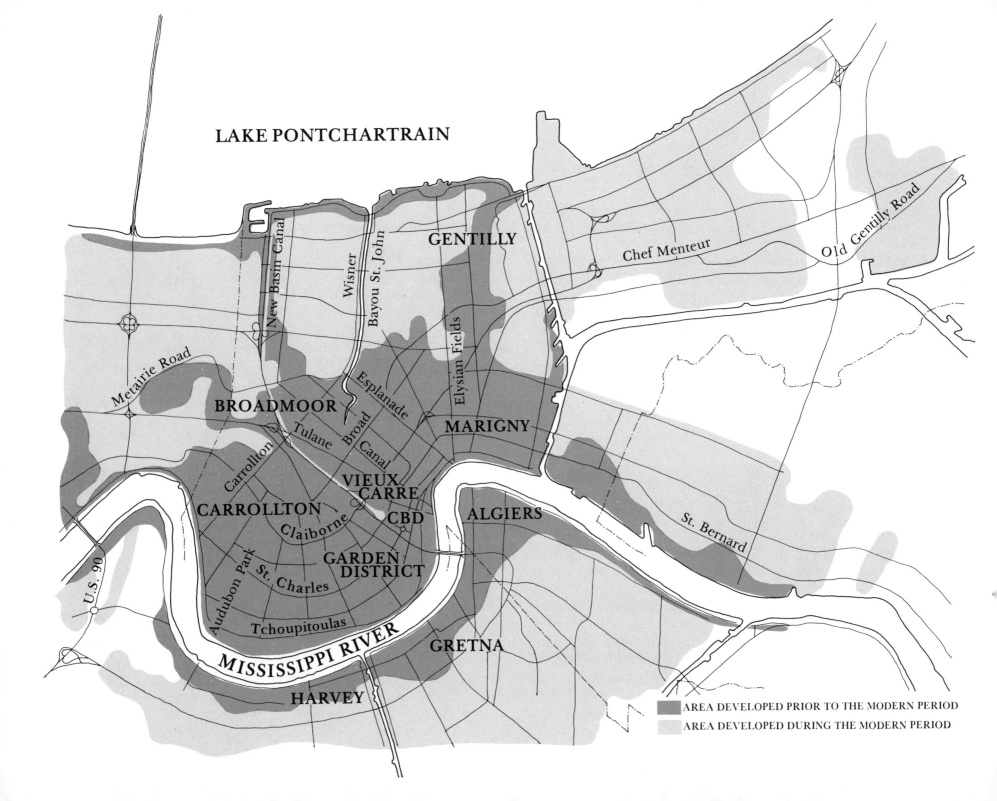

LAKE PONTCHARTRAIN

GENTILLY

Chef Menteur

Old Gentilly Road

New Basin Canal

Wisner

Bayou St. John

Metairie Road

Elysian Fields

Esplanade

BROADMOOR

Broad

Tulane

Canal

MARIGNY

Carrollton

VIEUX CARRE

CARROLLTON

Claiborne

CBD

ALGIERS

St. Bernard

Audubon Park

GARDEN DISTRICT

St. Charles

U.S. 90

Tchoupitoulas

MISSISSIPPI RIVER

GRETNA

HARVEY

■ AREA DEVELOPED PRIOR TO THE MODERN PERIOD
▨ AREA DEVELOPED DURING THE MODERN PERIOD

miles across Lake Pontchartrain into St. Tammany Parish, opening up a vast new area for suburban development on the north shore.

Suburban sprawl in the metropolitan area occurred very rapidly. As a result the newer areas do not have the variety of house styles common in older sections of the city that developed over longer periods of time and incorporated a mixture of styles. Most of the suburbs were developed with houses of a new style: Suburban Ranch. By the end of the sixties these houses had sprung up in eastern New Orleans, the Lakefront, Metairie, and the West Bank as well as in the surrounding parishes. However, the suburban exodus was not as sweeping as in some American cities, and many inner-city neighborhoods retained their vitality, thus preserving a large number of older houses.

Between 1950 and 1975, as the population of the city proper declined the developed metropolitan area nearly doubled in size, leaving very little vacant residential land except in New Orleans East and parts of Algiers on the West Bank. But by this time urban flight to the suburbs had greatly diminished and many parts of the inner city were experiencing a renaissance. Public appreciation of older neighborhoods was increasing, and houses suffering from years of neglect were restored or renovated.

Population growth continued until about 1980, when the census placed the city population at 557,482 and the metropolitan area population at 1.3 million. Economic decline in the 1980s, principally in the oil industry, resulted in a loss of population, particularly in New Orleans. The 1990 census count placed the population at just under 500,000 in the city, with 1.2 million people living in the greater metropolitan area.

THE INTERNATIONAL STYLE (1930–)

The modern movement in architecture emerged in Germany, Holland, and France in the 1920s, ushering in new design theories that have been with us to some degree ever since. The two major styles of the movement were Art Deco and the International style. Art Deco was never popularized in residential construction in New Orleans, although a number of commercial and institutional buildings were constructed in this style.

The philosophies of the International style were refined in the Bauhaus School in Dessau, Germany. The concept evolved around the relating of art and architecture to the new machine age, and had as its leading proponents Walter Gropius, Ludwig Mies van der Rohe, Le Corbusier, and J. J. P. Oud. It was this era that produced the streamlined designs still much in evidence today; cars, trains, furniture, and appliances were all designed for a futuristic effect.

The International style was introduced in the United States in the late 1920s with the construction of the Lovell "Health" House in Los Angeles, designed by Richard Neutra, an Austrian architect who had come to America in 1923. In the twenty or so years prior to its introduction, the U.S. had witnessed various revival movements. When the International style surfaced, historical eclecticism was abandoned.

The major characteristics of the style are stark simplicity, flexible planning, and the elimination of all ornament. Right angles dominate, and a feeling of functionalism is manifest in a form-follows-function design. Pure volume is the effect desired.

Roofs are normally flat, and smooth, uniform wall surfaces are marked by ribbons of windows articulated to appear as continuations of the wall rather than as holes piercing it. Often this effect is further accentuated by windows turning the corners of a house in a continuous band of glass with no visible structural support. Steel casement windows with multilights are frequently used, and it is not uncommon to find glass block worked into the design. Walls are generally smooth stucco, painted white, or vertical wood siding with flush, almost invisible joints. A general feeling of horizontality prevails, achieved primarily by bands of windows and flat roofs.

The wall house is another expression of the International style, inspired by the German pavilion designed by Ludwig Mies van der Rohe for the International Exposition in Barcelona, Spain, in 1929. The building featured an enclosure created by a series of walls pulled apart with large glass panes as infill. Some of the Usonian houses designed by Frank Lloyd Wright in the 1930s and 1940s also influenced this style, as did houses designed by Richard Neutra, who used large expanses of fixed glass and aluminum-frame sliding-glass doors extensively. A number of International-style wall houses were constructed in New Orleans; new ones are still constructed occasionally, generally in brick or stucco with flat roofs and a slight overhang, or in a very boxy version with no overhang.

INTERNATIONAL STYLE HOUSE

A two-story International-style house with smooth stucco walls, a flat roof, and multilight windows in steel frames. The windows run in horizontal bands, turning the corner of the building with no visible corner support. The entranceway is very simple and straightforward, with a paneled door beneath a small, semicircular projecting canopy and a glass-block opening above. The house is very boxlike, with no visible roof line or projecting eaves.

A one-story garage with a multipaneled door projects toward the front from the right side of the house.

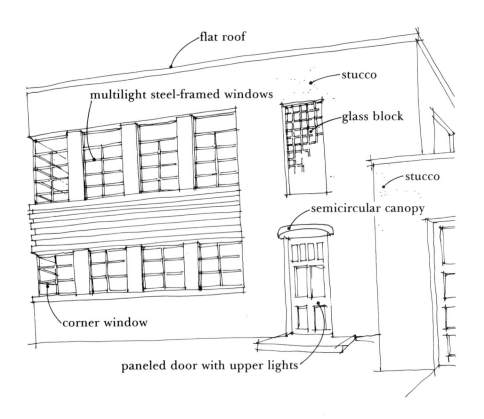

flat roof

stucco

multilight steel-framed windows

glass block

stucco

semicircular canopy

corner window

paneled door with upper lights

INTERNATIONAL STYLE WALL HOUSE

This International-style wall house takes its inspiration from the Barcelona Pavilion designed by Ludwig Mies van der Rohe in 1929. The idea is to create window fenestrations by separating walls rather than by cutting holes in walls. The openings created are filled in with fixed glass in wood mullions. (Frequently aluminum-frame sliding-glass doors are used in combination with large expanses of fixed glass to create entire walls of glass opening onto rear patios.)

The front entrance, reached by a long walkway protected by a generous roof overhang, consists of a single flush door with fixed-glass sidelights. A spacious two-car carport terminates the right front facade.

The house, constructed on a concrete slab on grade, has a flat roof with wide overhangs. Some houses of this style in New Orleans have very slight overhangs and some none at all, creating a more boxlike appearance.

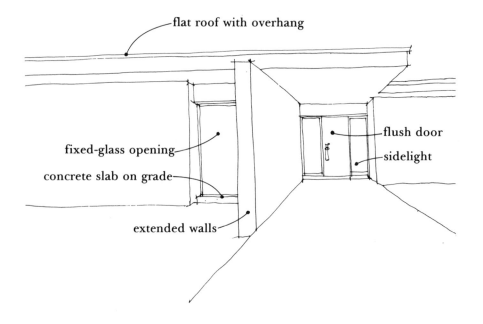

flat roof with overhang

fixed-glass opening

concrete slab on grade

extended walls

flush door

sidelight

THE SUBURBAN RANCH STYLE (1945–)

The large majority of houses built since the 1940s may be categorized as Suburban Ranch. The style was strongly influenced—not so much in detailing as in concept—by the Prairie School houses of Frank Lloyd Wright, which were built on concrete slabs on grade, expressing a low, horizontal feeling, with generous roof overhangs and carports. Although many Suburban Ranch houses were built in urban areas, they established their strongest foothold in the new suburbs that sprang up throughout the country after World War II.

One of the major characteristics unique to the style is its emphasis on the importance of the automobile. Single and double garages and carports command attention, an example of the influence of cultural values on design. Another new characteristic is the relationship of the house to the ground. The great majority of Suburban Ranch houses are built on concrete slabs, no more than twelve inches above grade, thus coming full circle from the placement of the first colonial houses built more than two hundred years earlier.

Floor plans vary greatly. The houses are most often rectangular or L-shaped, with hipped or gabled roofs and sometimes both. Ceiling heights, which had been getting lower for some time, now reached the national standard of eight feet.

Aluminum, double-hung windows with insect screens are the rule. Shutters are often utilized as decorative elements only, and are generally of a size that would not fit the windows they border even if they were hinged and could be closed. A large fixed-glass picture window in the front facade was a popular feature during the 1950s and 1960s. The 1970s witnessed the proliferation of various period motifs including classical, French colonial, and Spanish colonial, as well as a return to attached townhouses, popular for the first time in over a hundred years.

Front yards are important features of Suburban Ranch houses. Siting in most cases accentuates the low horizontal look. Brick veneer over wood-frame construction was an answer to the search for low maintenance, but as yards grew in size and prestige they generated a new maintenance requirement: the large, manicured front lawn.

With the advent of television, people began to abandon the front porch for the den, and air conditioning kept them there, especially during the summer months. Eventually the front porch disappeared entirely from new residential construction.

SUBURBAN RANCH HOUSE

A one-story brick-veneer Suburban Ranch house on a concrete slab on grade. A low-pitched, hipped roof has a projecting overhang and enclosed soffits (roof rafters are rarely left exposed in the overhang).

A large garage with a paneled door projects very visibly from the left facade and is reached by a concrete driveway. A concrete walk leads to the recessed entrance, which has a flush door flanked by full-length, fixed-glass sidelights. The windows are aluminum, six-over-six, and double-hung. (In the Suburban Ranch style aluminum double-hung windows are by far the most common type; they are generally one-over-one, two-over-two, or six-over-six.) The house illustrated here does not have shutters, although they are a common feature—almost always used as decoration only.

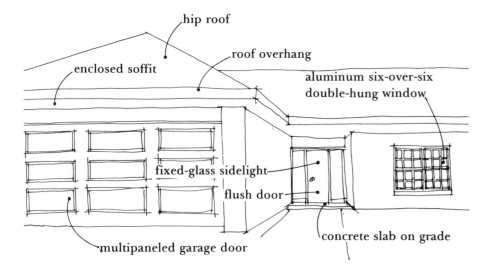

hip roof

enclosed soffit

roof overhang

aluminum six-over-six
double-hung window

fixed-glass sidelight

flush door

multipaneled garage door

concrete slab on grade

GLOSSARY

ABAT-VENT—A roof extension, almost flat, supported by iron bearers and cantilevered from the facade at the roof line.

ACANTHUS—A prickly herb of the Mediterranean region; leaves of the acanthus were used for designs in classical ornamentation.

APPLIQUÉ—Applied ornament.

ARCADE—A series of arches supported by columns or piers.

ARCH—A curvilinear structural opening.

ARCHITRAVE—The lowest part of an entablature.

ATTIC—All the space under a pitched roof of a building.

BALCONY—A platform projecting from an upper level of a building and surrounded by a railing.

BALUSTER—A shaftlike element used to support a handrail.

BALUSTRADE—A railing (such as a porch railing) made up of rails, balusters, and posts.

BANQUETTE—Sidewalk.

BARGEBOARD—An ornamental board attached to the projected eave of a gable roof.

BARREL TILE—A half-cylinder–shaped clay roof tile.

BAYS—Repetitive divisions into which a building is divided.

BEADED BOARD—A board with a rounded edge separated from the rest of the board by a small depression.

BEAM—A horizontal supporting member.

BEVELED GLASS—Glass with beveled edges, held together by lead strips. Popular in the Victorian era.

BOUSILLAGE—A construction method for walls using a mixture of mud and moss as infill between heavy timber posts.

BRACKET—A support element under eaves, balconies, or other over- hangs. Frequently used as ornamentation rather than for struc- tural support.

BRICK MASONRY—Construction technique using bricks held to- gether by mortar.

BRICK VENEER—A wall of brick covering an inner wall such as a wood frame.

BRIQUETE-ENTRE-POTEAUX—A construction method for walls using brick as infill between heavy timber posts.

CABINET—A small room situated in the rear outer corner of certain house types, primarily French colonial, Creole cottages, and American cottages.

CAPITAL—The uppermost part of a column or pilaster.

CARPORT—An open-sided shelter for automobiles.

CASEMENT WINDOW—A window that opens on hinges like a door; a common window type in colonial New Orleans.

CASING—An enclosing frame around a door or window opening.

CAST IRON—Iron shaped by placement in a mold, used for railing, fences, etc.

CHAIN WALL—A continuous foundation raising a house off the ground.

CLAPBOARD—*See* Weatherboard.

CLASSICAL ARCHITECTURE—The architecture of Greece and Rome during the pre-Christian era.

COLONNADE—A series of columns at regular intervals, supporting a covered passageway.

COLONNETTES—Slender, turned wooden columns.

COLUMN—A vertical support normally consisting of a base, a round shaft, and a capital. The Greek Doric order is exceptional in that it has no base.

COLOMBAGE—Construction consisting of heavy timber framework mortised and tenoned together and covered with wide hori- zontal boards. A common construction method in New Orleans during the early colonial period.

CORINTHIAN ORDER—The most ornate of the classical Greek orders, characterized by a bell-shaped capital decorated with acanthus leaves.

CORNICE—The upper, projecting section of an entablature or ornamental molding along the top of a building.

COURTYARD—An enclosed open-air space next to a building.

CREOLE—A person descended from French and/or Spanish colonists. Also a style of architecture prevalent during the postcolonial period in New Orleans.

CRESTING—Ornamentation occurring at an upper limit, such as the ridge of a roof.

DENTILS—Closely spaced blocks in Greek Ionic and Corinthian cornices.

DIMENSIONAL LUMBER—Lumber cut at sawmills.

DORIC ORDER—The simplest of the classical Greek orders, distinguished by columns with unadorned capitals and no bases.

DORMER—A projection from a wall or roof structure. When it rises from a roof it is called a roof dormer and when it is an extension of a wall it is called a wall dormer.

DOUBLE—A two-family house.

DOUBLE-HUNG WINDOW—A window type introduced to New Orleans in the early 1800s, consisting of two sashes that operate through vertical movement.

DROP SIDING—A type of weatherboard with a depression in the upper part of each board.

EAVE—The projecting overhang of a roof.

EGG-AND-DART—Decorative molding consisting of alternating egg- and dart-shaped elements.

ENTABLATURE—In classical architecture, the horizontal part of a classical order supported by columns or pilasters and consisting of the architrave, the frieze, and the cornice.

ENTRESOL—A low floor used for storage between the ground floor and an upper floor; a Spanish colonial characteristic.

ETCHED GLASS—Glass with a design produced by the process of exposure to acid.

EYEBROW ROOF DORMER—A low, curvilinear roof dormer resembling the shape of an eye, used on some Richardsonian Romanesque buildings.

FACADE—The front wall of a building.

FANLIGHT—A fan-shaped or semicircular window over a door or window with radiating muntins.

FAUBOURG—A French word meaning suburb.

FENESTRATIONS—The window and door openings in a building.

FINIAL—The topping ornament of a roof gable, turret, baluster, post, etc.

FIRE WALL—A brick wall extending above the roof line between attached buildings, intended to prevent a fire from spreading from one building to another.

FISH-SCALE SHINGLES—Wooden shingles cut in a shape to resemble fish scales. Popular during the Victorian era.

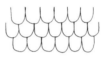 FISH-SCALE SHINGLES

FIXED GLASS—A glass pane that is stationary, rather than operable.

FLAGGED—Paved with flagstones.

FLAT-HEADED WINDOW—A window whose uppermost part is horizontal.

FLUTING—Closely spaced, parallel, vertical channeling on the shaft of a column or pilaster.

FRENCH DOORS—A pair of hinged doors, generally with glass lights.

FRIEZE—The middle part of a classical entablature.

GABLE—The triangular upper part of a wall formed by a pitched roof.

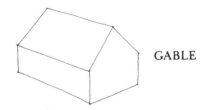 GABLE

GALLERY—Exterior space under the main roof of a house. *Compare* Porch.

GOTHIC ARCH—A pointed arch. A major characteristic of the Gothic style.

GRADE—Ground level.

GREEK KEY—An overlapping lintel over a doorway with a slight flaring out of the face of the doorway surround from the top to the bottom.

GREEK KEY

GRILLE—A grating forming a barrier or screen.

HALF-TIMBERING—A method of wall construction in which the wooden structural members are exposed on the exterior wall with stucco infill between.

HIPPED ROOF—A roof with four uniformly sloped sides.

HIPPED ROOF

HOOD MOLDS—A shallow projected covering used over doors and windows in the Italianate style.

IONIC ORDER—An order of classical Greek architecture, characterized by columns with a scroll-like capital.

JACK ARCH LINTEL—A door or window lintel constructed with splayed bricks.

JIGSAW WORK—Decorative woodwork, generally curvilinear in shape, common in the Victorian era and produced by the use of a jigsaw.

JOIST—A beam supporting a floor or a ceiling.

LEADED GLASS—Small panes of glass—clear, beveled, or stained—held together by lead strips.

LEVEE—An embankment to prevent flooding.

LIGHT—A glass pane in a window or door.

LINTEL—The horizontal structural element above a window or door, usually carrying the wall load above.

MANSARD ROOF—A roof with a double slope on all four sides, the lower slope much steeper than the upper.

MANSARD ROOF

MILLWORK—Woodwork shaped or dressed by means of a rotary cutter.

MODILLIONS—Small bracketlike ornamentation under the cornice of a classical entablature.

MOLDING—A linear decorative element, or curved strip, used for ornamentation or trimwork.

MORTAR JOINTS—The exposed joints of mortar in masonry.

MORTISE AND TENON—A construction technique that joins two wooden members by the projection of one member to fit securely into a corresponding cavity cut in the other.

MULTILIGHT—Having many lights or glass panes, as a window or door.

PALLADIAN WINDOW—A window consisting of three parts, a central semicircular window flanked by smaller, square-headed windows on each side.

PARAPET—A low wall or railing along the edge of a roof.

PEAK FINIAL—An ornament at the peak of a roof.

PEDESTAL—A support for a column.

PEDIMENT—A low-pitched gable in the classical manner; also used in miniature over doors or windows.

PEDIMENT

PICTURE WINDOW—A large, fixed-glass window in the facade of a house. Common in Suburban Ranch houses in the 1950s and 1960s.

PIER—A square support for a house.

PIERCEWORK—Ornamentation common in the Late Victorian period, created by cutting openings in various shapes in a solid piece of wood.

PILASTER—A column attached to a wall.

PILLAR—A square or rectangular upright support.

PITCH—The angle or slope of a roof.

PLASTER—A composition of lime, water, and sand, that is soft when applied and hardens upon drying; used for coating and finishing walls and ceilings.

PORCH—Exterior space attached to a house, but with a separate roof. *Compare* Gallery.

PORTE COCHERE—A covered entrance for the passage of vehicles.

PORTICO—A covered entrance to a building.

POST—A structural member, usually wood, set in an upright position and used as a support; a pillar; also, the structural element supporting a balustrade.

QUOIN—A stone, brick, or wood block used to accentuate the outside corners of a building.

RAILS—A metal enclosure generally used for porches, galleries, and balconies.

RAFTER—A sloping structural member of a pitched roof.

ROSETTE—A round decorative element in a floral motif.

ROSETTE

ROUND-HEADED WINDOW—A window whose uppermost part is rounded.

ROW HOUSES—Single-family houses attached and constructed in rows.

RUSTICATION—Rough-surfaced stonework, most commonly found on Richardsonian Romanesque houses.

SASH—The wood frame of a window in which the glass panes are set.

SCROLLWORK—Ornamentation in the form of scrolls.

SEGMENTAL-ARCH HEAD—The uppermost part of a door or window constructed in the shape of a segment of a circle.

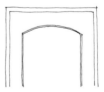

SEGMENTAL-ARCH HEAD

SHED ROOF—A roof that is pitched in only one direction.

SHINGLES—A wall or roof covering, consisting of small overlapping pieces, square or patterned.

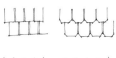

 SHINGLES

SHUTTER—A hinged movable cover, usually of wood, for a window or door.

SIDELIGHTS—Stationary glass panes flanking an entrance door.

SIDING—The material used to cover the exposed side of a wood-frame building (weatherboard, drop siding, etc.).

SILL—A horizontal member forming the lowest portion of a building or window; also, the bottom of a door.

SINGLE—A one-family house.

SLIDING WINDOW—A window with one or more sashes sliding horizontally on a track; similar in operation to a sliding glass door.

SOFFIT—The underside of a roof overhang.

SPANISH CONSOLE—A wrought-iron bracket projecting from a wall and supporting a balcony.

SPINDLE—A turned decorative wooden element.

SPRING POINT—The point at which an arch starts.

SQUARE-HEADED WINDOW—A window whose uppermost part is horizontal, at ninety degrees to the sides.

STAINED GLASS—Colored glass.

STILTED ARCH—An arch with a straight extension below a segmental arch, used in the Italianate style.

 STILTED ARCH

STRAP HINGES—Hinges, used primarily on shutters and gates, that are attached to the face instead of the side. Used primarily in the colonial and postcolonial periods.

STUCCO—Exterior plaster.

SURROUNDS—The framework and associated trim around a door or window.

SWAGS—Classical ornamentation resembling evergreen branches hanging in a curve between two points.

SYRIAN ARCH—A semicircular arch with short support elements.

TRANSOM—A glazed opening over a door or window.

TRUSS—An assemblage of structural members forming a rigid structural framework.

TUDOR GOTHIC ARCH—A pointed arch in the Gothic manner, but lower and wider.

TURNED WOOD—Wooden elements such as spindles or balusters produced by being turned on a lathe.

TURRET—A small tower, usually at the corner of a building, extending above the roof line and often housing a stairway; most commonly found on Queen Anne houses.

VIEUX CARRE—The old quarter of New Orleans as it was laid out by the early French settlers.

VOLUTE—Spiral- or scroll-shaped ornament.

WEATHERBOARD—A long, narrow board, usually slightly thicker at one edge, used for siding; applied horizontally and slightly overlapping. Also referred to as clapboard.

WEATHERBOARD

WOOD FRAME—Refers to a building whose structural elements are composed of a wood frame constructed of small dimensional lumber and held together with nails.

WROUGHT IRON—Iron worked into shape by manual effort; used for balcony railings, fences, gates, hardware, lanterns, etc.

BIBLIOGRAPHY

Basso, Etolia S. *The World from Jackson Square; A New Orleans Reader.* New York: Farrar, Straus and Company, 1948.

Benjamin, Asher. *The American Builder's Companion.* Unabridged reprint of the sixth edition. New York: Dover Publications, 1969.

Bowra, C. M., and the editors of Time-Life Books. *Classical Greece.* New York: Time Incorporated, 1965.

Bruce, Curt. *The Great Houses of New Orleans.* New York: Alfred A. Knopf, 1977.

Cable, Mary. *Lost New Orleans.* Boston: Houghton Mifflin Company, 1980.

Chase, John C.; Cowan, Walter G.; Dufour, Charles L.; LeBlanc, O. K.; and Wilds, John. *New Orleans, Yesterday and Today.* Baton Rouge: Louisiana State University Press, 1983.

Christovich, Mary Louise; Evans, Sally Kittredge; and Toledano, Roulhac. *New Orleans Architecture : The Creole Faubourgs.* Gretna: Pelican Publishing Company, 1974.

Christovich, Mary Louise; Holden, Pat; Swanson, Betsy; and Toledano, Roulhac. *New Orleans Architecture: The American Sector.* Gretna: Pelican Publishing Company, 1972.

Christovich, Mary Louise, and Iseley, N. Jane. *New Orleans Interiors.* New Orleans: Friends of the Cabildo, Louisiana State Museum, and The Historic New Orleans Collection, 1980.

Downing, A. J. *The Architecture of Country Houses.* Reprint of the original 1850 edition. New York: Dover Publications, 1969.

Flaherty, Carolyn. "The Colonial Revival House." *The Old House Journal,* January 1978.

Fletcher, Sir Banister. *A History of Architecture on the Comparative Method.* New York: Charles Scribner's Sons, 1963.

Fossier, Albert Emile. *New Orleans.* New Orleans: Pelican Publishing Company, 1957.

Glassie, Henry. *Pattern in the Material Folk Culture of the Eastern United States.* Philadelphia: University of Pennsylvania Press, 1968.

Gowans, Alan. *Images of American Living: Four Centuries of Architecture and Furniture as Cultural Expressions.* Philadelphia: J. B. Lippincott, 1964.

Hamlin, Talbot. *Greek Revival Architecture in America.* New York: Dover Publications, 1964.

Higginbotham, Jay. *Fort Maurepas: The Birth of Louisiana.* Mobile, Alabama: Griffice Printing Co., 1968.

Huber, Leonard V. *New Orleans: A Pictorial History.* New York: Crown Publishers, 1971.

Kahn, Renee. "The Bungalow Style." *The Old House Journal,* January 1978.

––––––. "The Queen Anne Style." *The Old House Journal,* January 1977.

Leavitt, Mel. *A Short History of New Orleans.* San Francisco: Lexikos, 1982.

Lewis, Pierce F. *New Orleans: The Making of an Urban Landscape.* Cambridge, Massachusetts: Ballinger Publishing Company, 1976.

Million, Henry A. *Key Monuments of the History of Architecture.* New Jersey: Prentice Hall, and New York: Harry N. Abrams.

New Orleans Chapter of the American Institute of Architects. *A Guide to New Orleans Architecture.* New Orleans: New Orleans Chapter of the American Institute of Architects, 1974.

Ochsner, Jeffery Karl. *H. H. Richardson: Complete Architectural Works.* Cambridge, Massachusetts: The M.I.T. Press, 1982.

Osmond, Edward. *Houses.* New York: The MacMillan Company, 1956.

Pevsner, Nikolaus. *An Outline of European Architecture.* Harmondsworth, England: Penguin Books, 1966.

Poppeliers, John; Chambers, Allen S.; and Schwartz, Nancy B. *What Style Is That?* Washington, D.C.: The Preservation Press of the National Trust for Historic Preservation, 1977.

Pothorn, Herbert. *Architectural Styles.* New York: The Viking Press, 1971.

Readers Digest Association, Inc. *The Story of America.* Pleasantville, New York: Readers Digest Association, 1975.

Reid, Richard. *The Book of Buildings.* New York: Van Nostrand Reinhold Company, 1983.

Rifkind, Carole. *A Field Guide to American Architecture.* New York: The New American Library, 1980.

Steegman, John. *Victorian Taste: A Study of the Arts and Architecture from 1830 to 1870.* Cambridge, Massachusetts: The M.I.T. Press, 1971.

Van Rensselaer, Mariana Griswold. *Henry Hobson Richardson and His Works.* Unabridged republication of a limited 1888 edition. New York: Dover Publications, 1969.

Ware, William R. *The American Vignola: A Guide to the Making of Classical Architecture.* New York: W. W. Norton & Company, 1977.

Whiffen, Marcus. *American Architecture Since 1780: A Guide to the Styles.* Cambridge, Massachusetts: The M.I.T. Press, 1969.

Williams, Henry Lionel, and Williams, Ottalie K. *A Guide to Old American Houses 1700–1900.* South Brunswick, New York: A. S. Barnes and Company, 1962.

Wilson, Samuel, Jr., and Lemann, Bernard. *New Orleans Architecture: The Lower Garden District.* Gretna: Pelican Publishing Company, 1971.